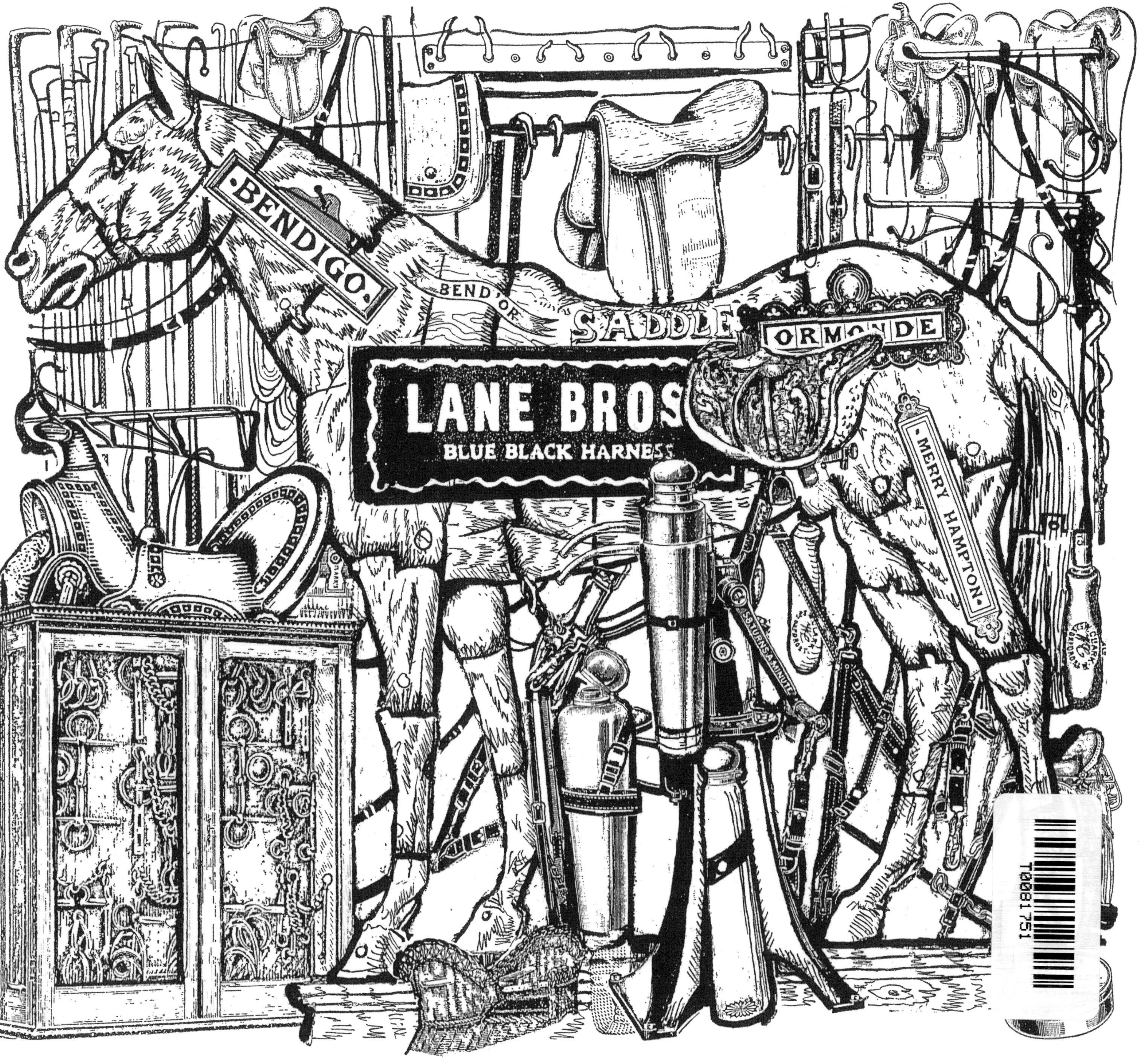
BENDIGO
BEND'OR
SADDLE
ORMONDE
LANE BROS
BLUE BLACK HARNESS
MERRY HAMPTON

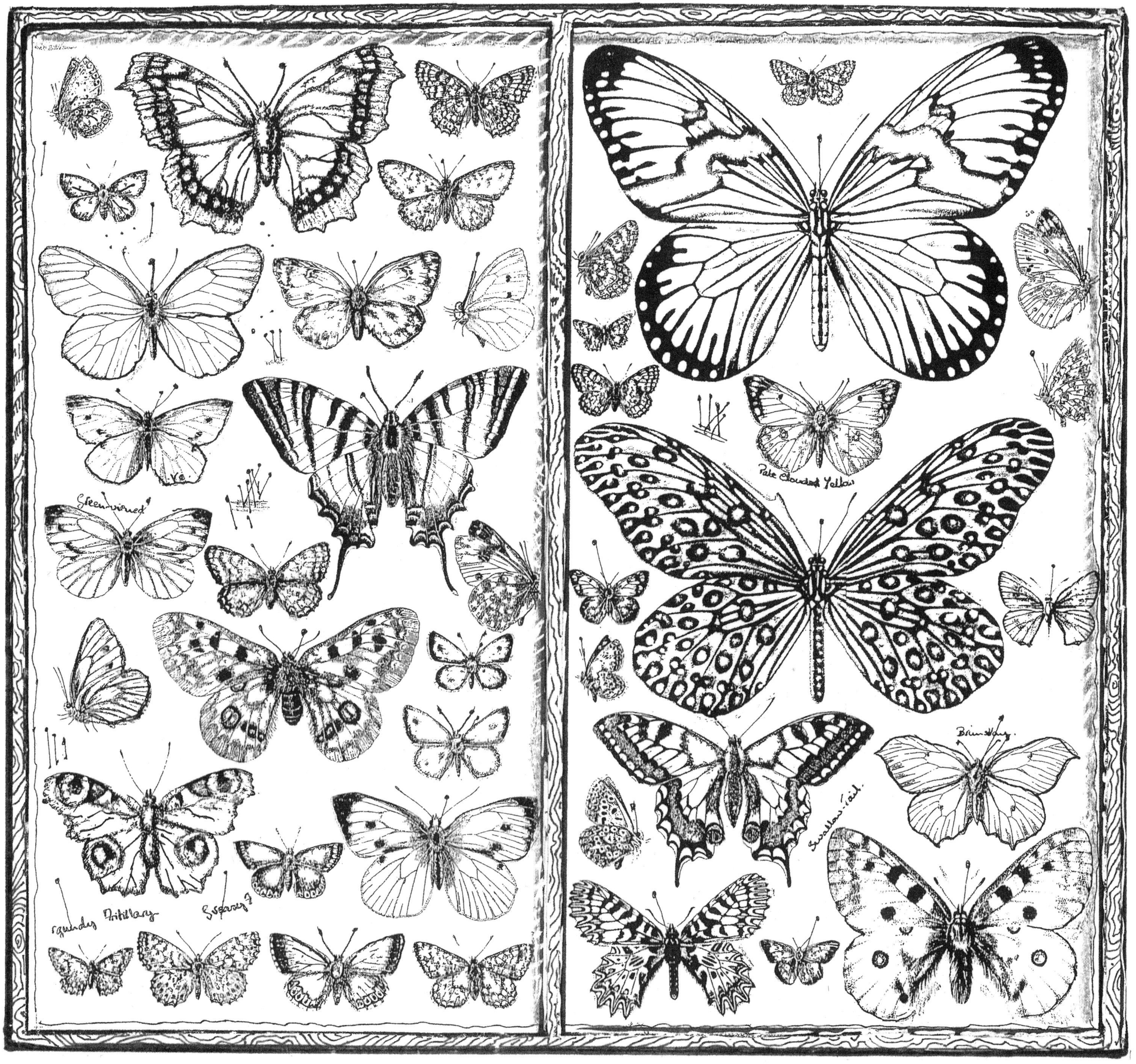
Green-veined
Pale Clouded Yellow
Brimstone
Swallow-tail
Fritillary

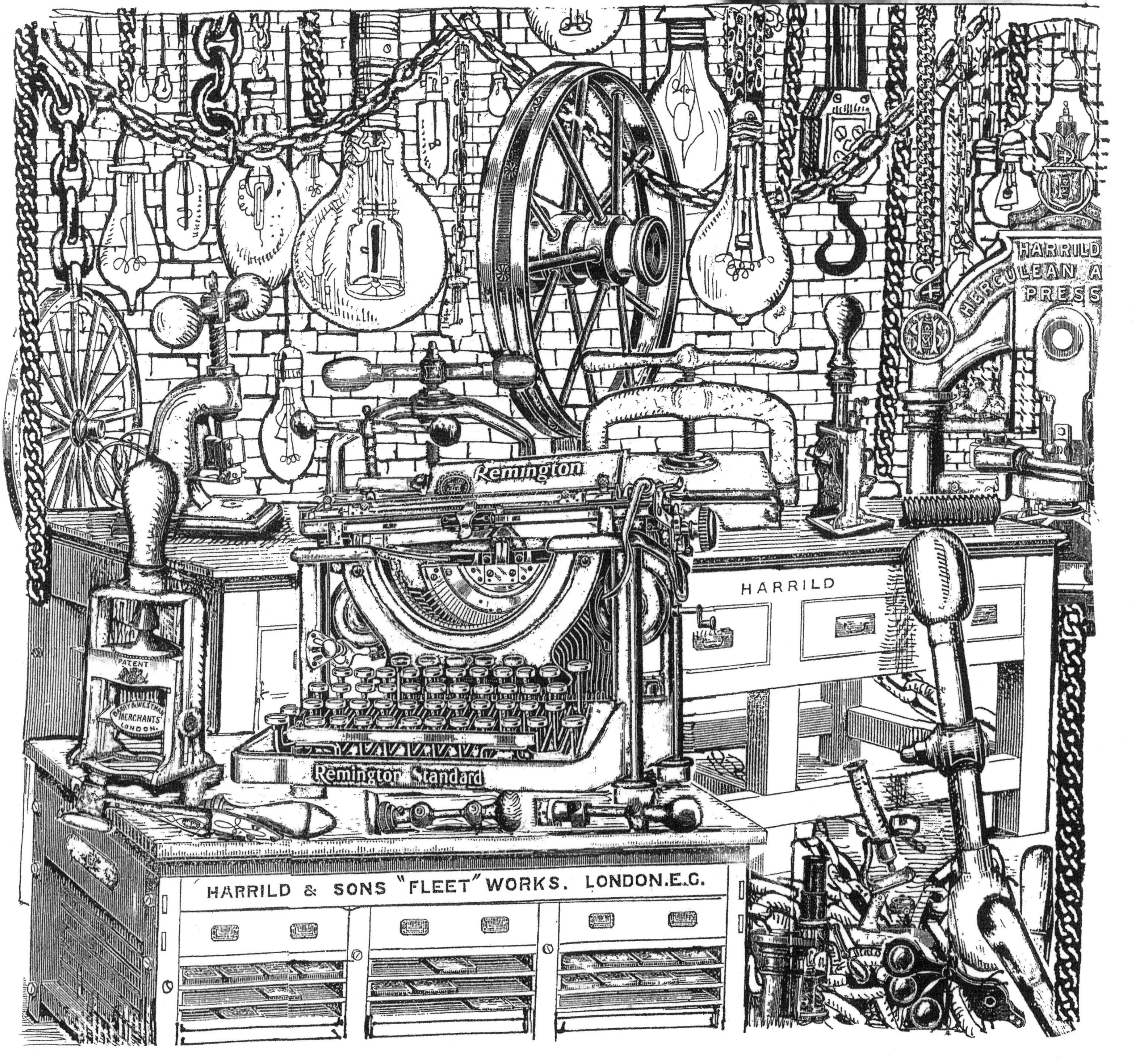

Remington
HARRILD
HERCULEAN A
PRESS
HARRILD
PATENT
BARRY & WESTMAN
MERCHANTS
LONDON.
Remington Standard
HARRILD & SONS "FLEET" WORKS. LONDON.E.C.

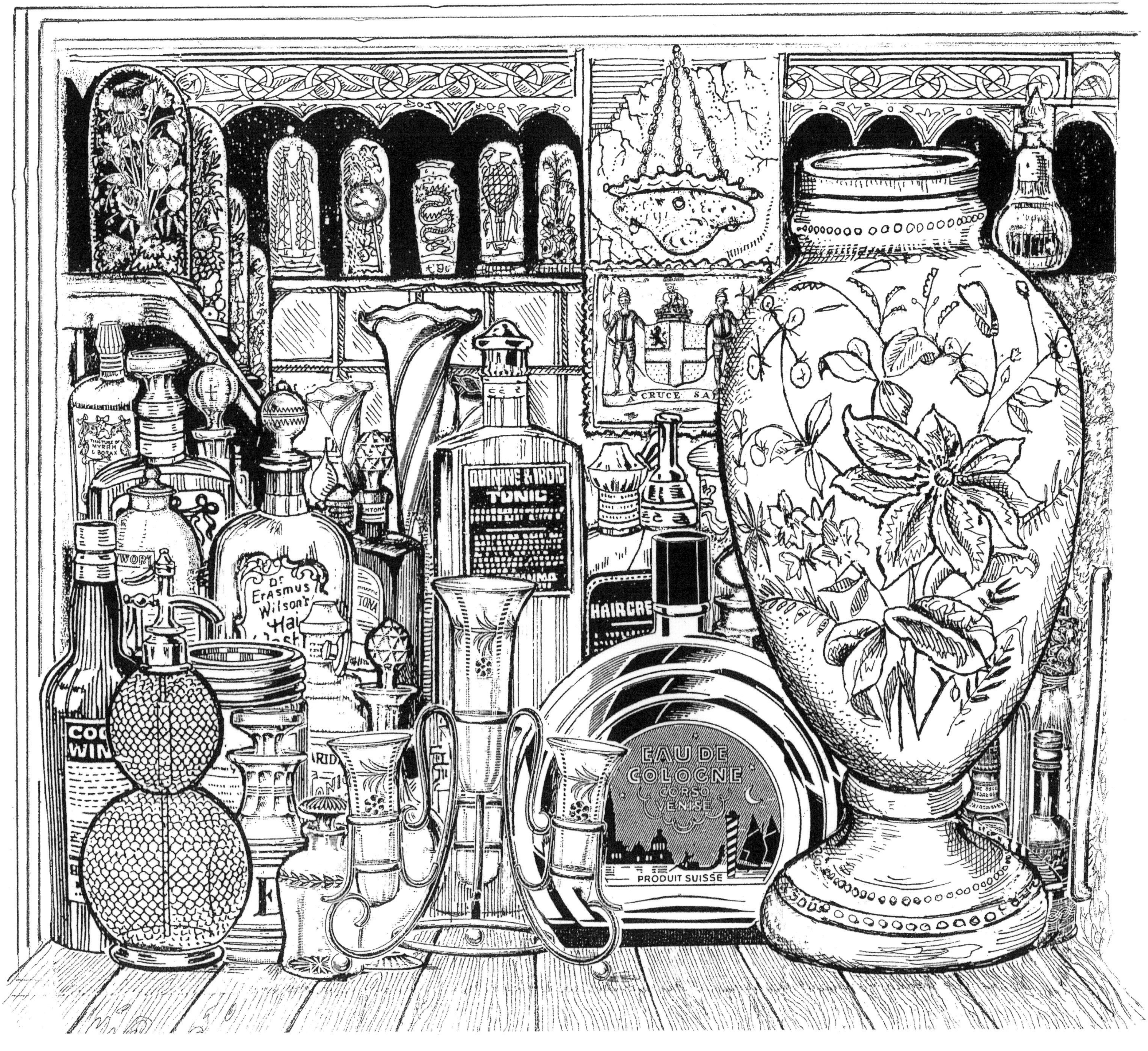
QUININE & IRON
TONIC
Dr Erasmus
Wilson's
HAIRCRE
A CRUCE SA
EAU DE
COLOGNE
CORSO
VENISE
PRODUIT SUISSE

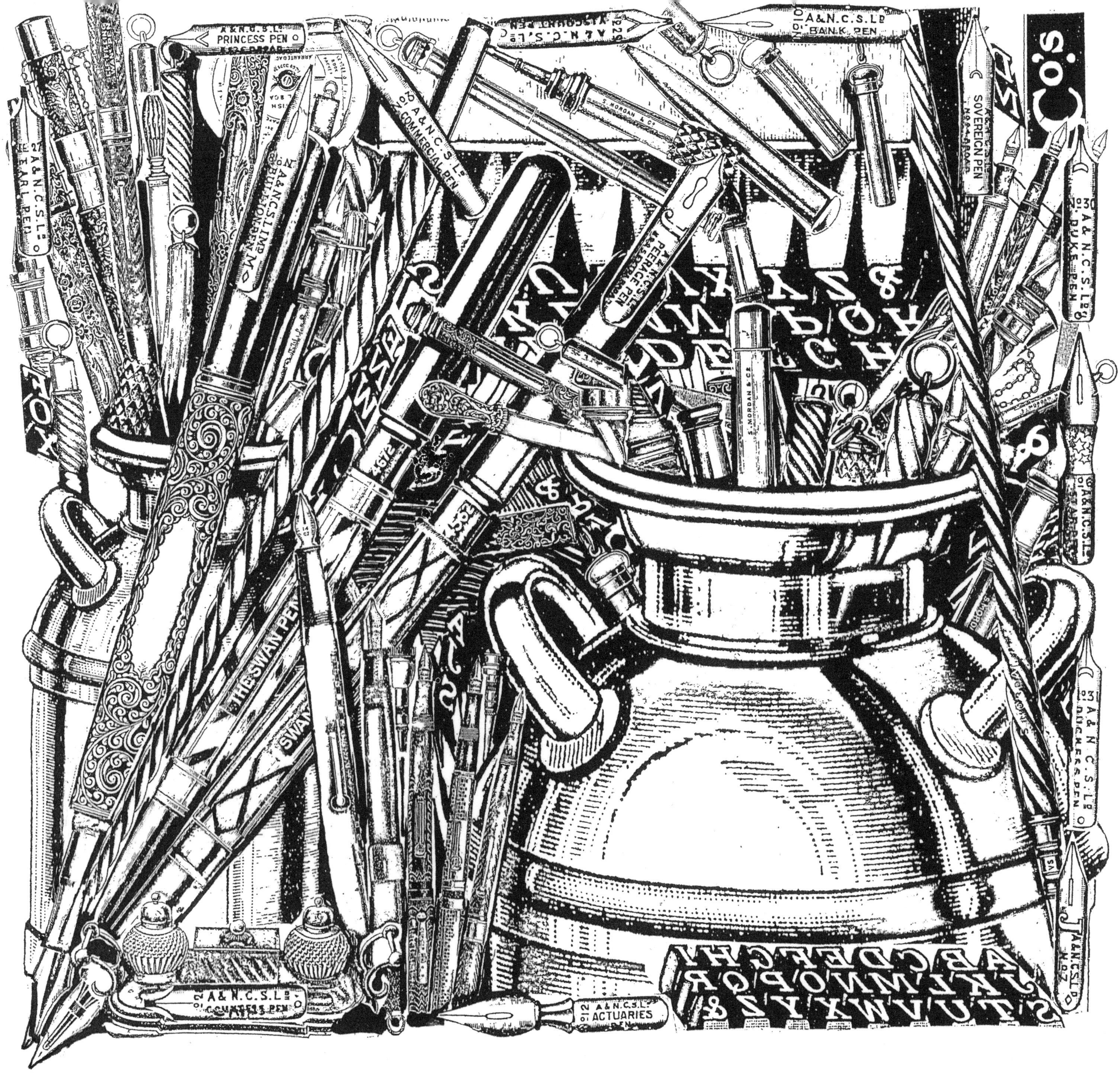
A & N. C. S. Ld
PRINCESS PEN
A&N.C.S.LD
BANK PEN
No 3 A & N.C.S.Ld
COMMERCIAL PEN
S. MORGAN & Co
SOVEREIGN PEN
A&N.C.S.Ld
PEERAGE PEN
No 30 A & N. C. S. Ld
DUKE PEN
A & N. C. S. Ld
EARL PEN
THE SWAN PEN
SWAN
No 31 A & N. C. S. Ld
DUCHESS PEN
No 12 A & N. C. S. Ld
ACTUARIES PEN
A & N. C. S. Ld
COUNTESS PEN
ABCDEFGHI
JKLMNOPQR
STUVWXYZ&

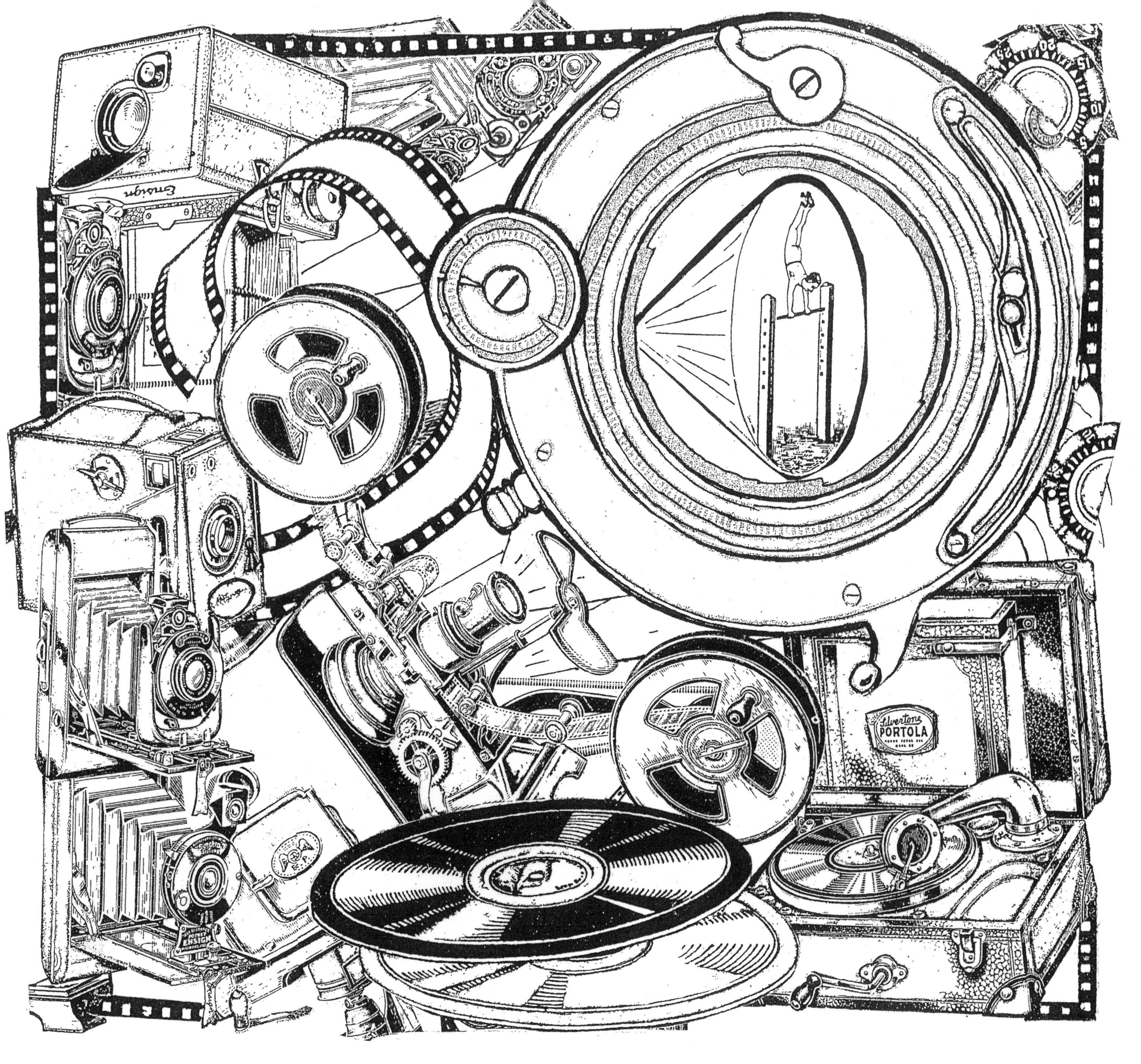
Silvertone
PORTOLA

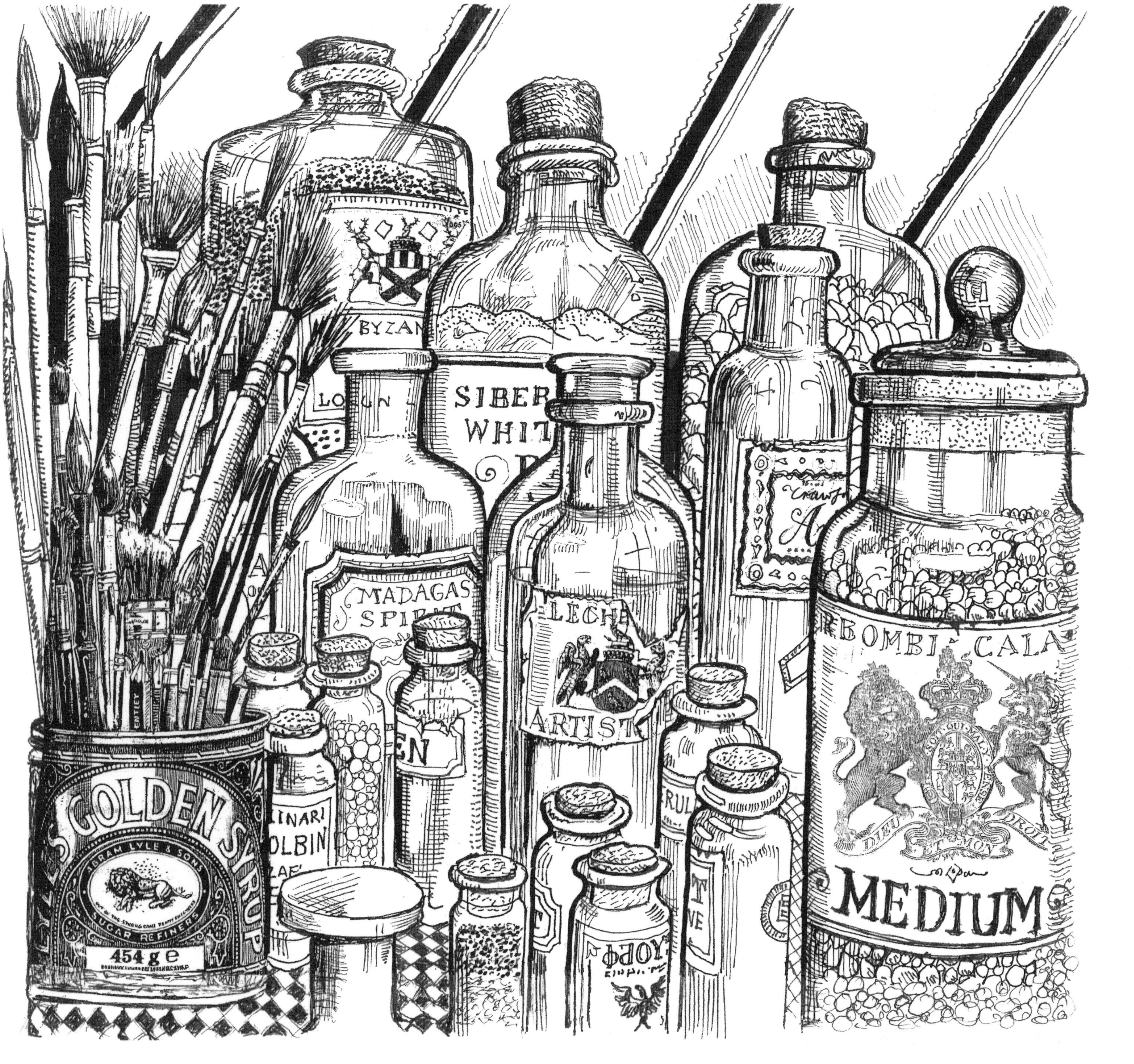

BYZAN
SIBER
WHIT
MADAGAS
SPIRIT
ARTIST
MEDIUM
DIEU
ET MON
DROIT
GOLDEN SYRUP
ABRAM LYLE & SONS
SUGAR REFINERS
454 g e

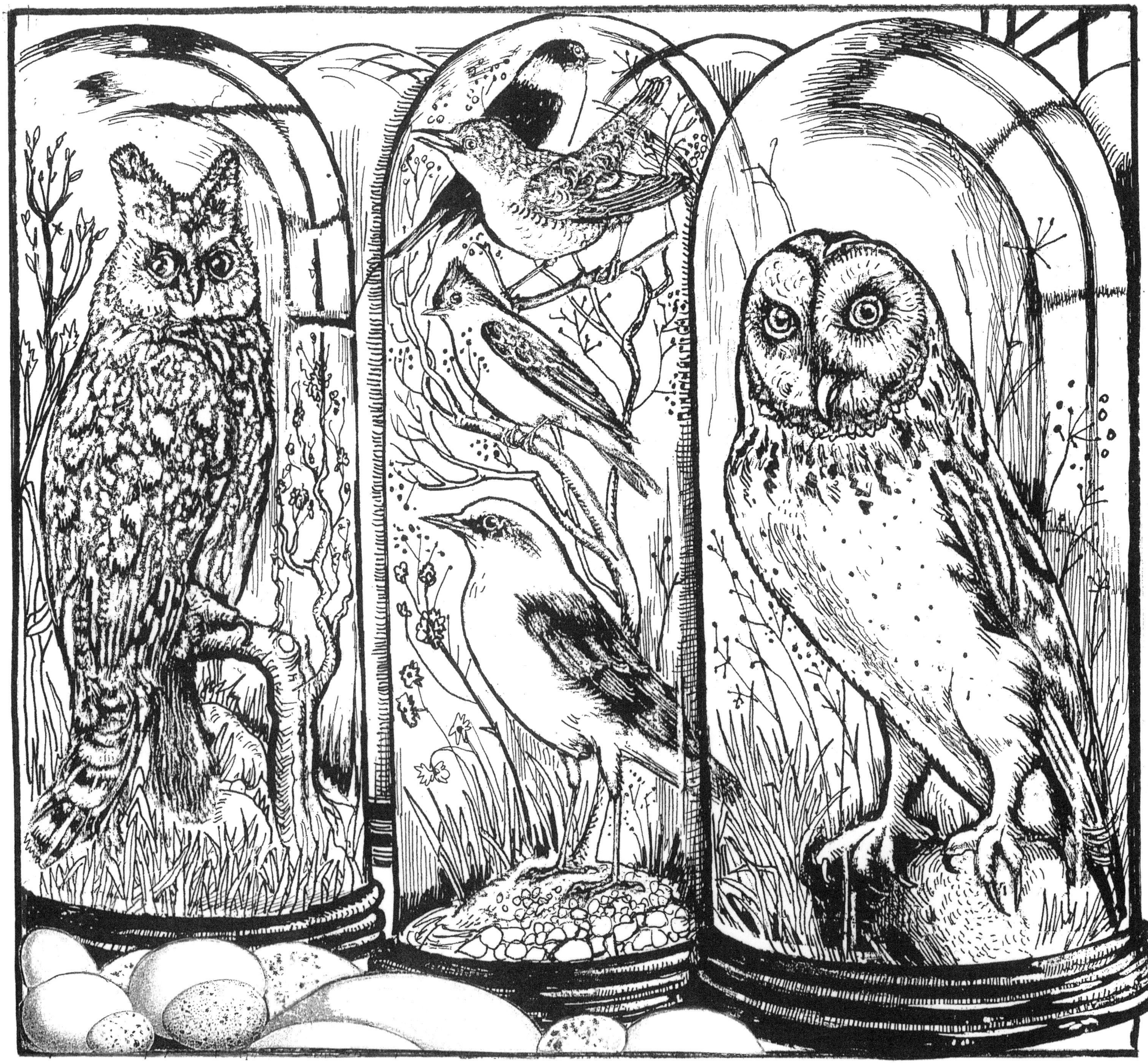

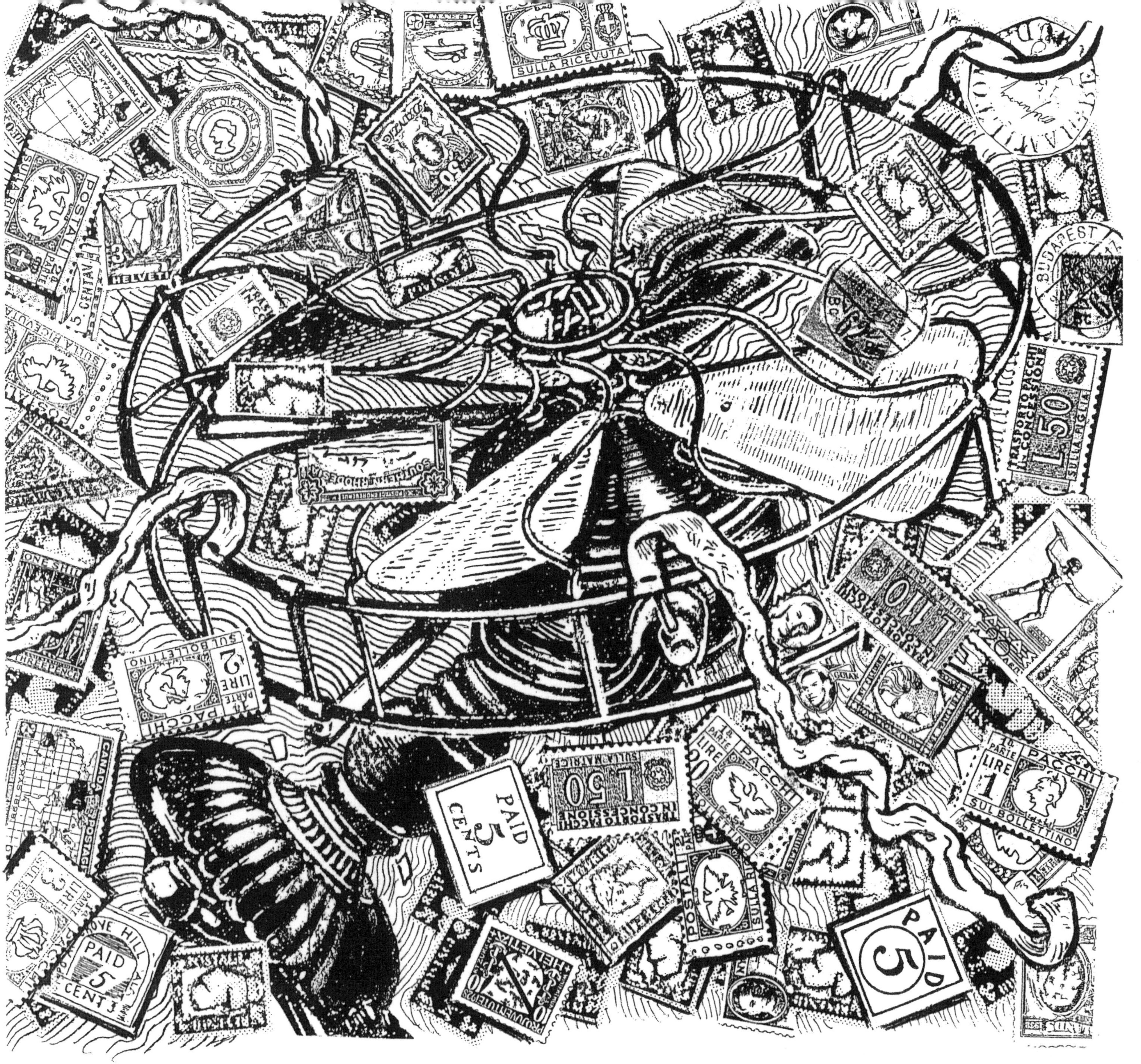

SULLA RICEVUTA
VAN DIEMEN'S LAND
FOUR PENCE
HELVETIA
BUDAPEST
TRASPORTO PACCHI
IN CONCESSIONE
PAID
5
CENTS
PACCHI
LIRE
1
SUL BOLLETTINO
CANADA POSTAGE
PAID
5

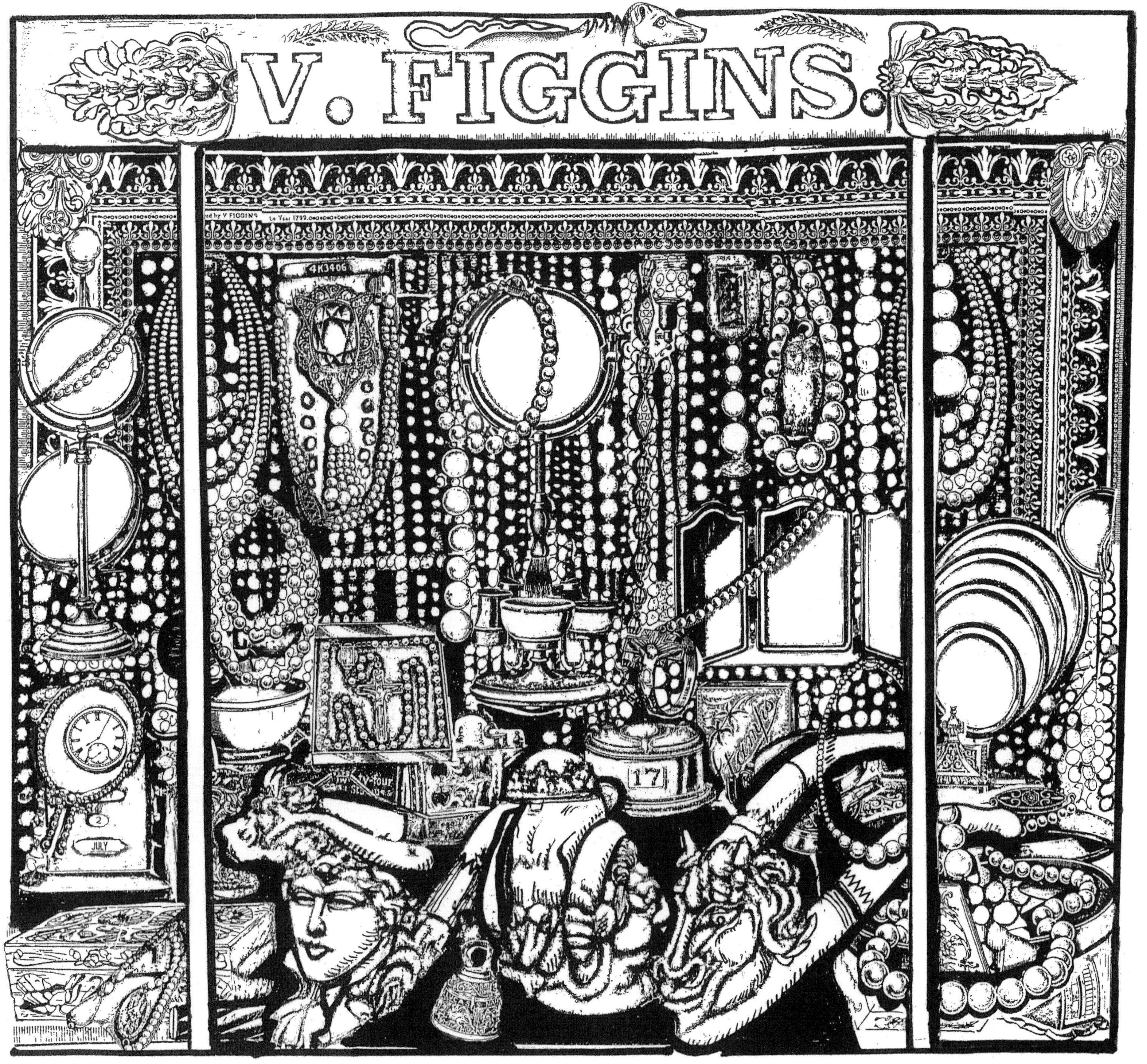
V. FIGGINS.
4K3406
17
2
JULY

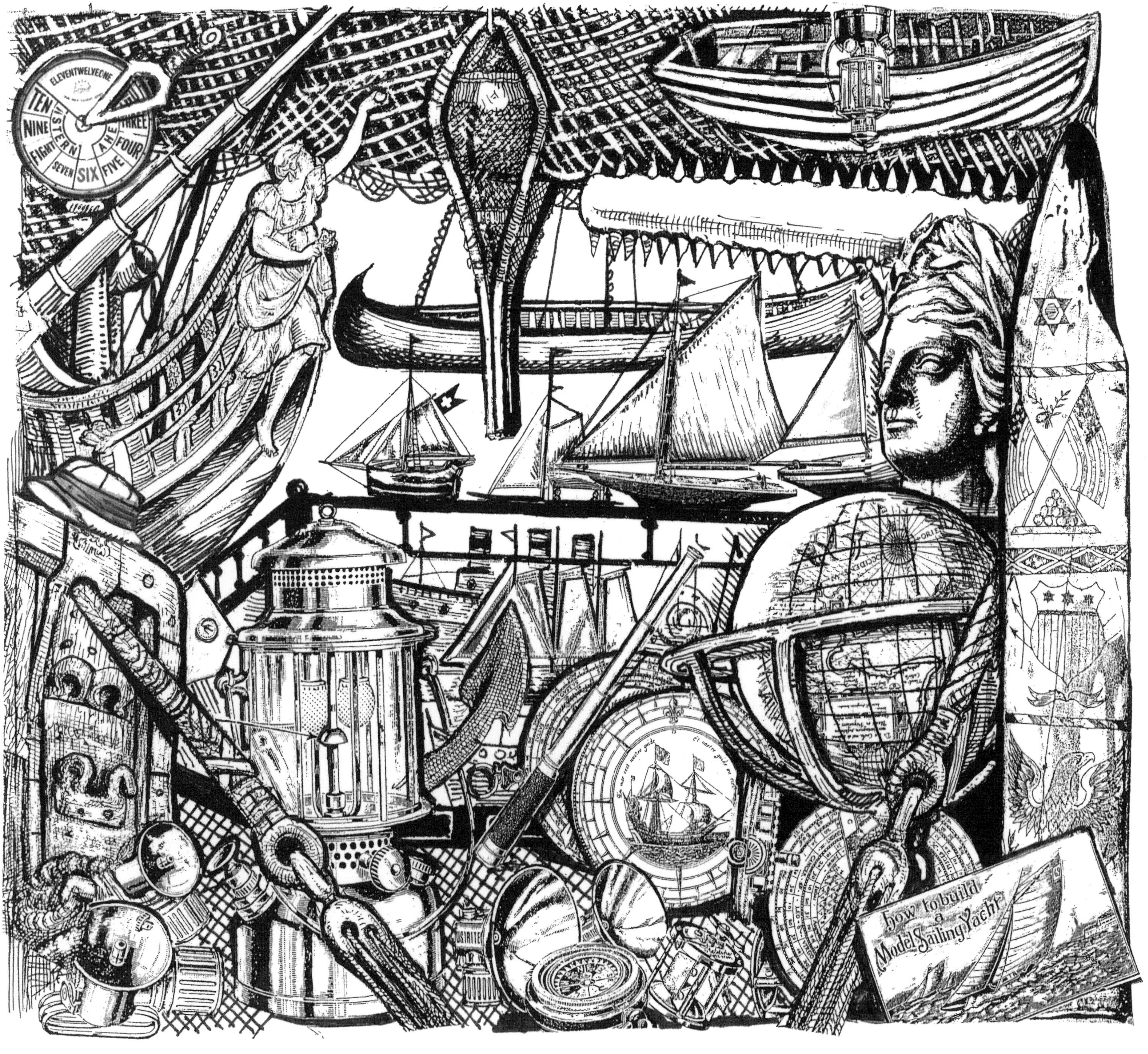

ELEVENTWELVEONE
TEN
NINE
EIGHT
STERN
SEVEN
SIX
FIVE
FOUR
THREE
How to build a Model Sailing Yacht

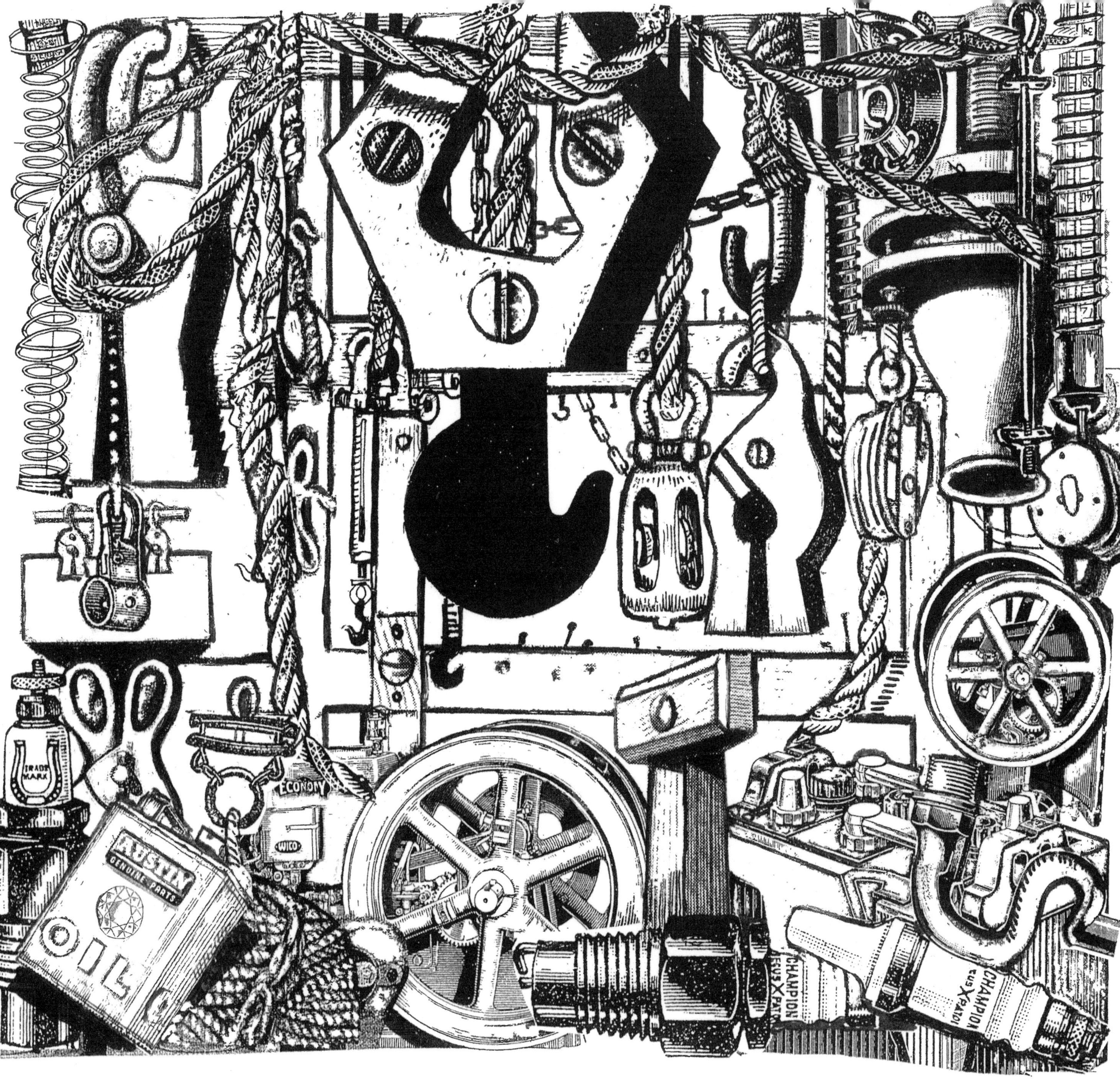
TRADE MARK
ECONOMY
WICO
AUSTIN
GENUINE PARTS
OIL
CHAMPION
CHAMPION

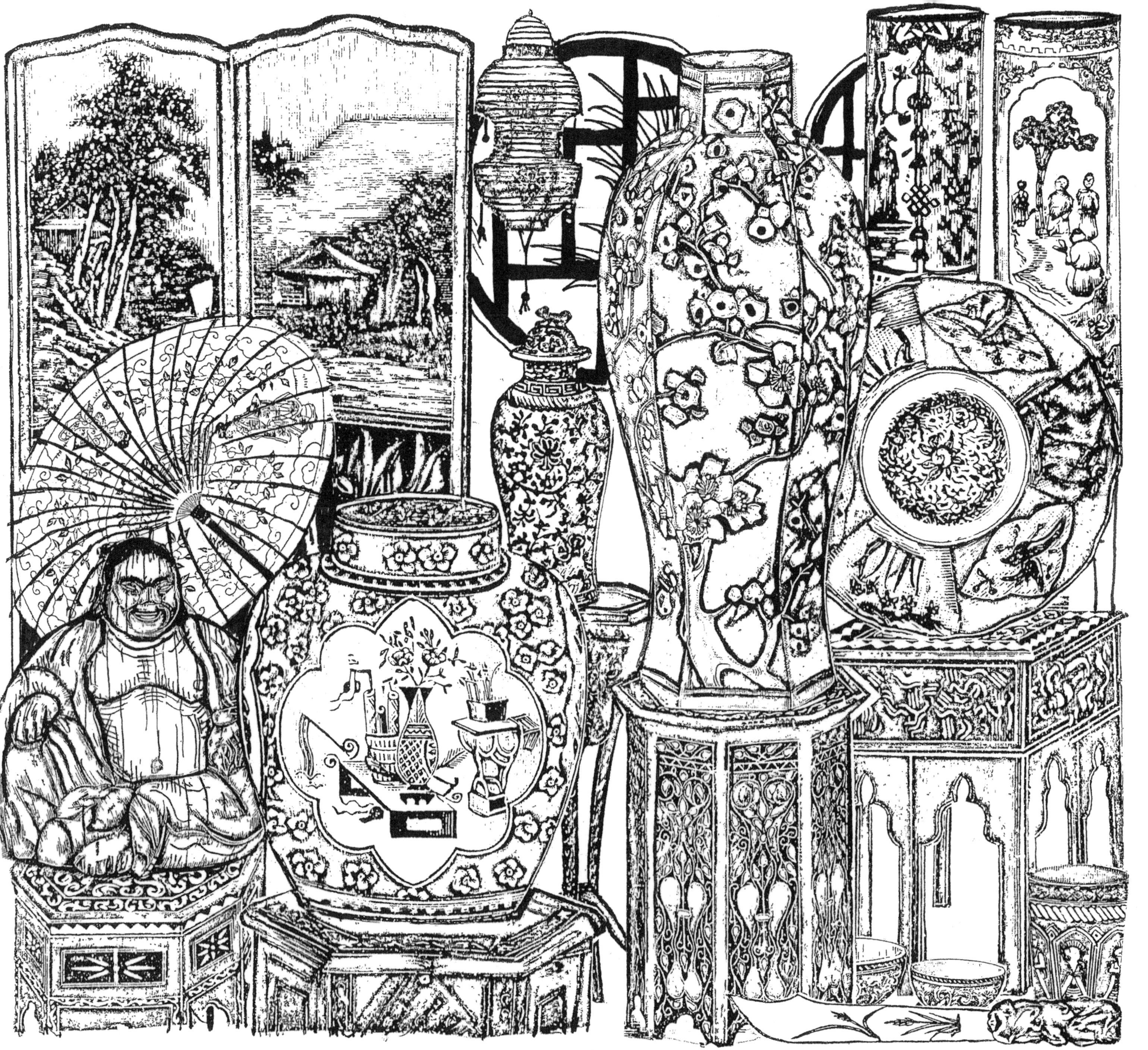

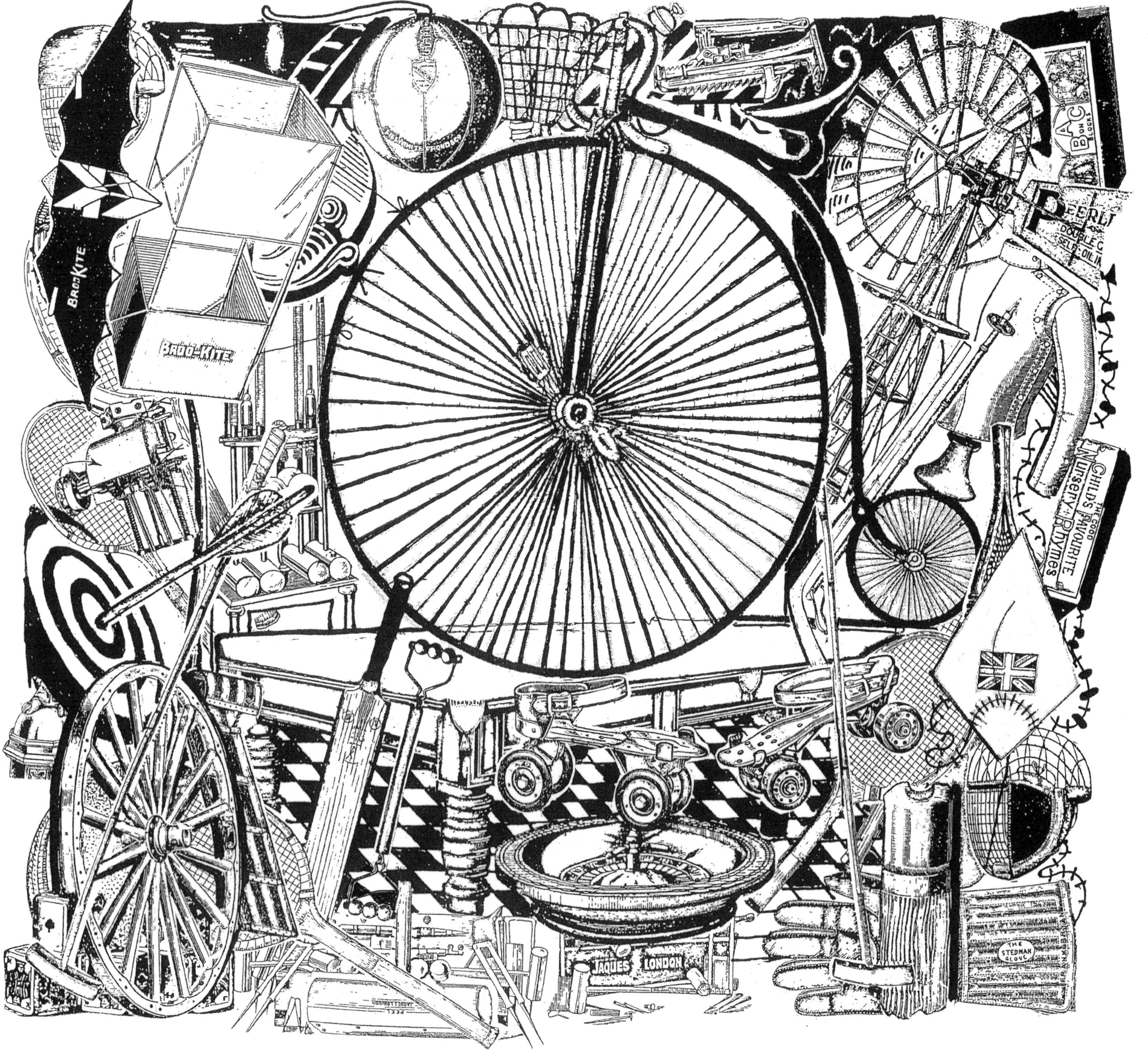
BROO-KITE
THE GOOD CHILD'S FAVOURITE Nursery Rhymes
JAQUES LONDON
THE STEDMAN GLOVE

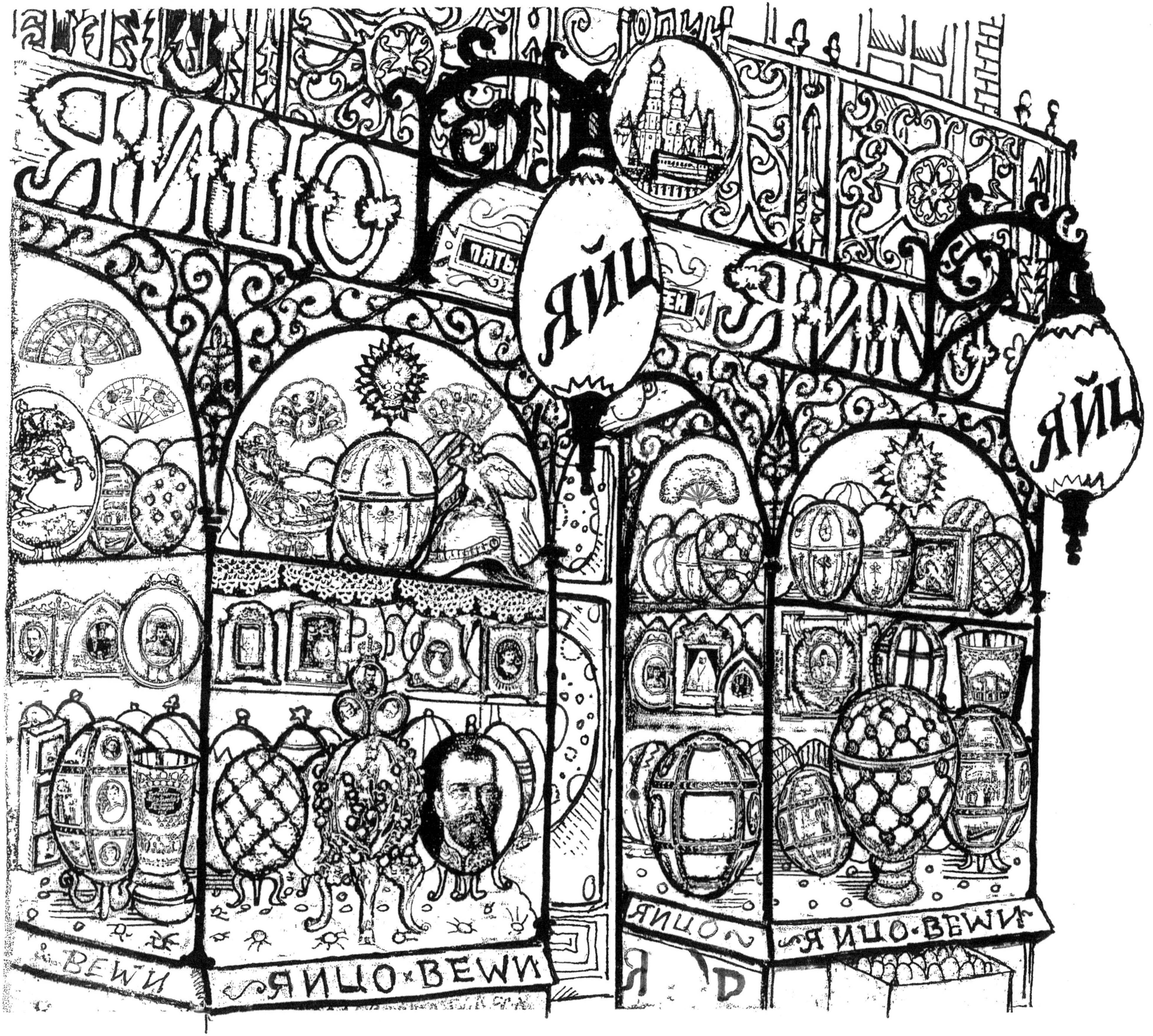
ПЯТЬ
ЯЙЦ
ЯЙЦ
ЯИЦО • ВЕЩИ

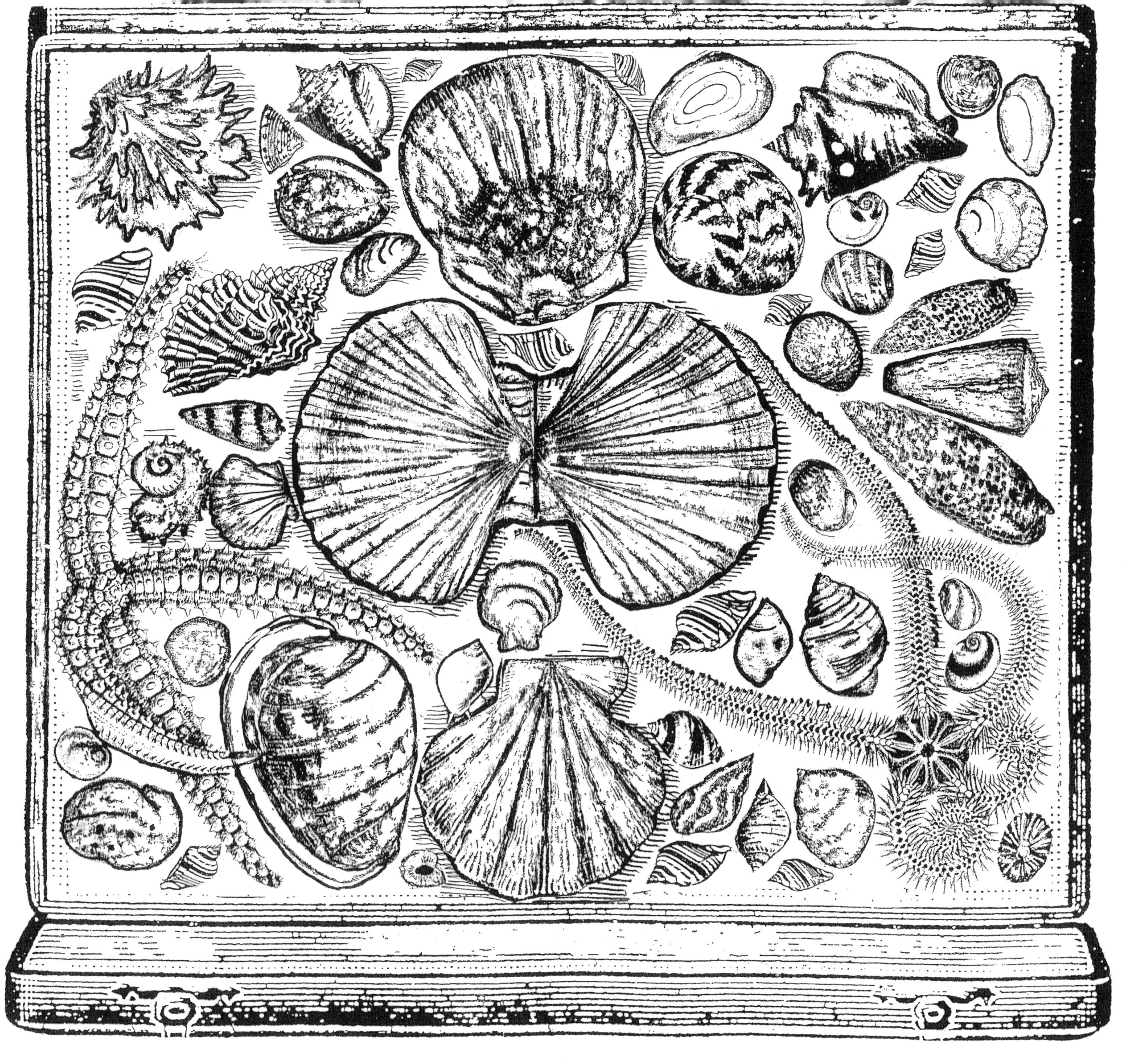

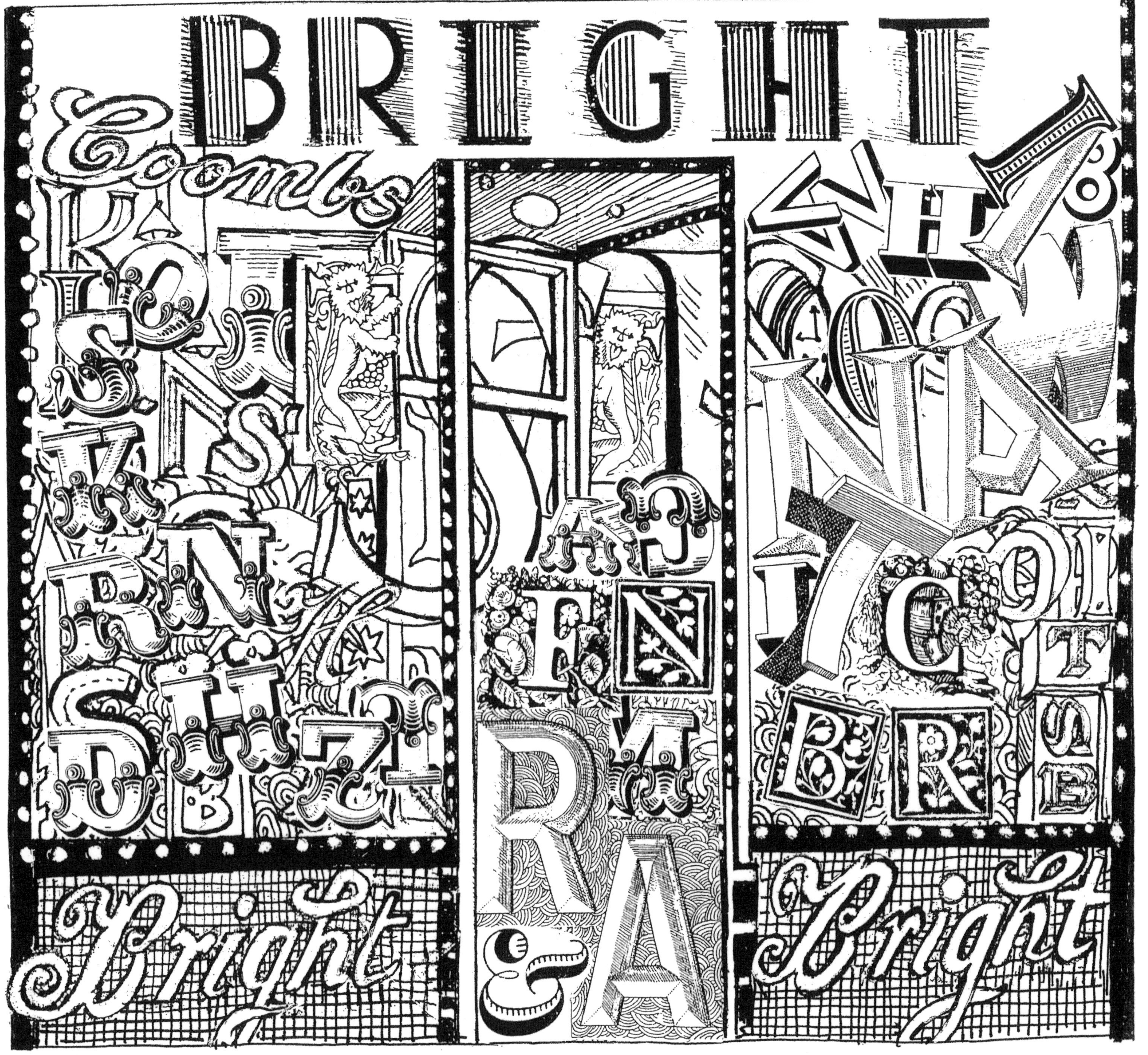
BRIGHT
Coombs
Bright
Bright

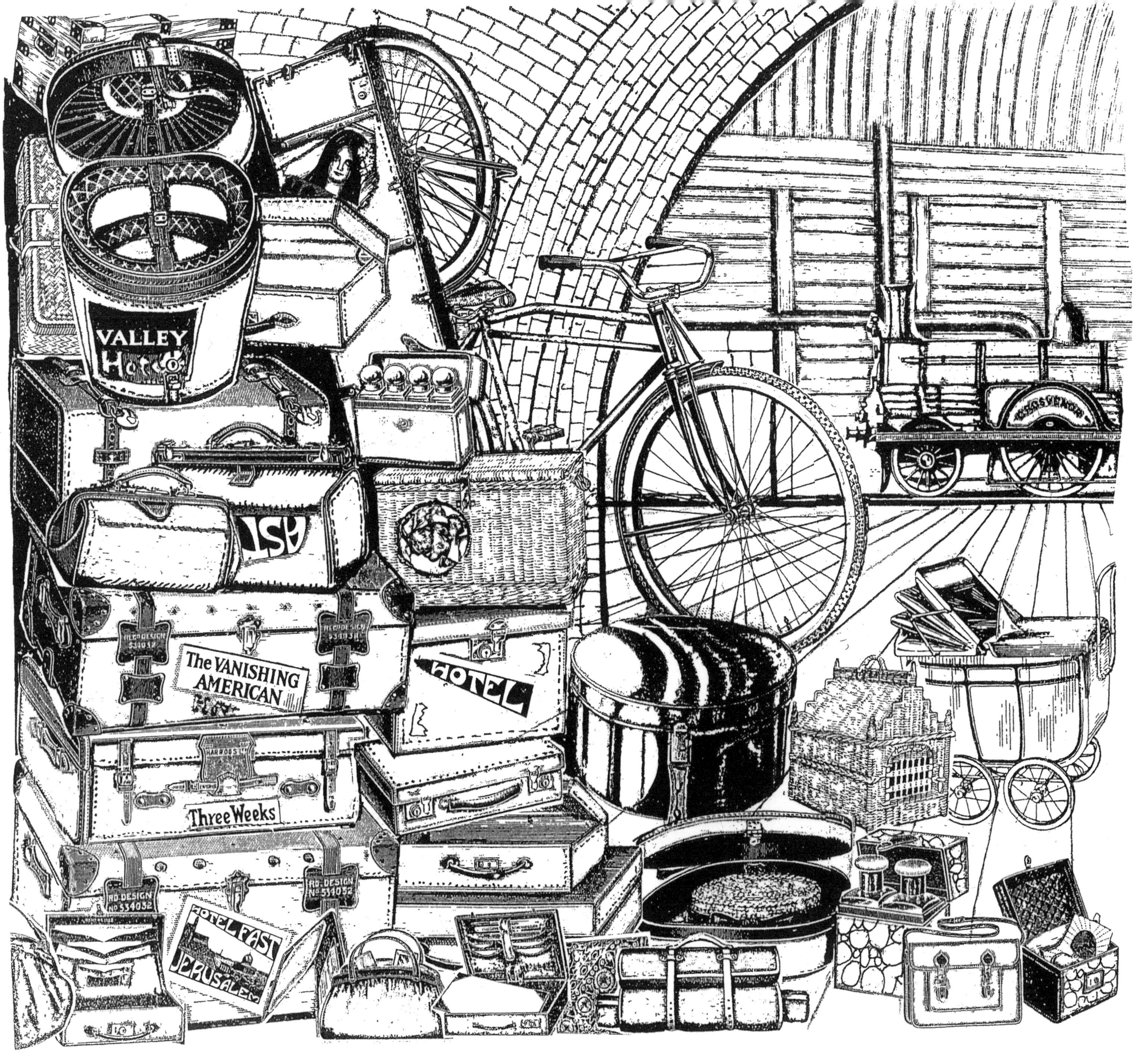
VALLEY
Hotel
The VANISHING AMERICAN
HOTEL
Three Weeks
HOTEL FAST
JERUSALEM

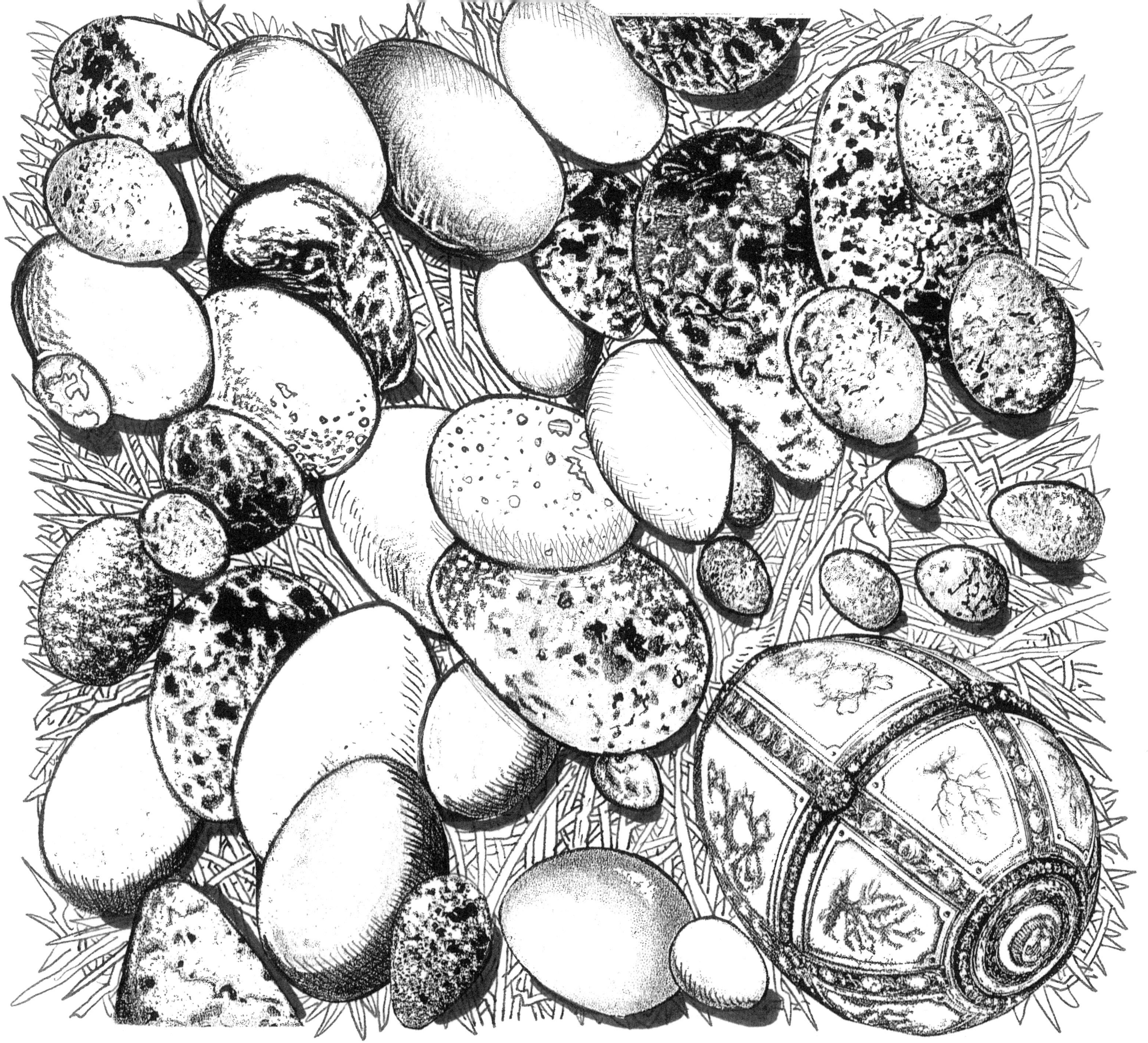

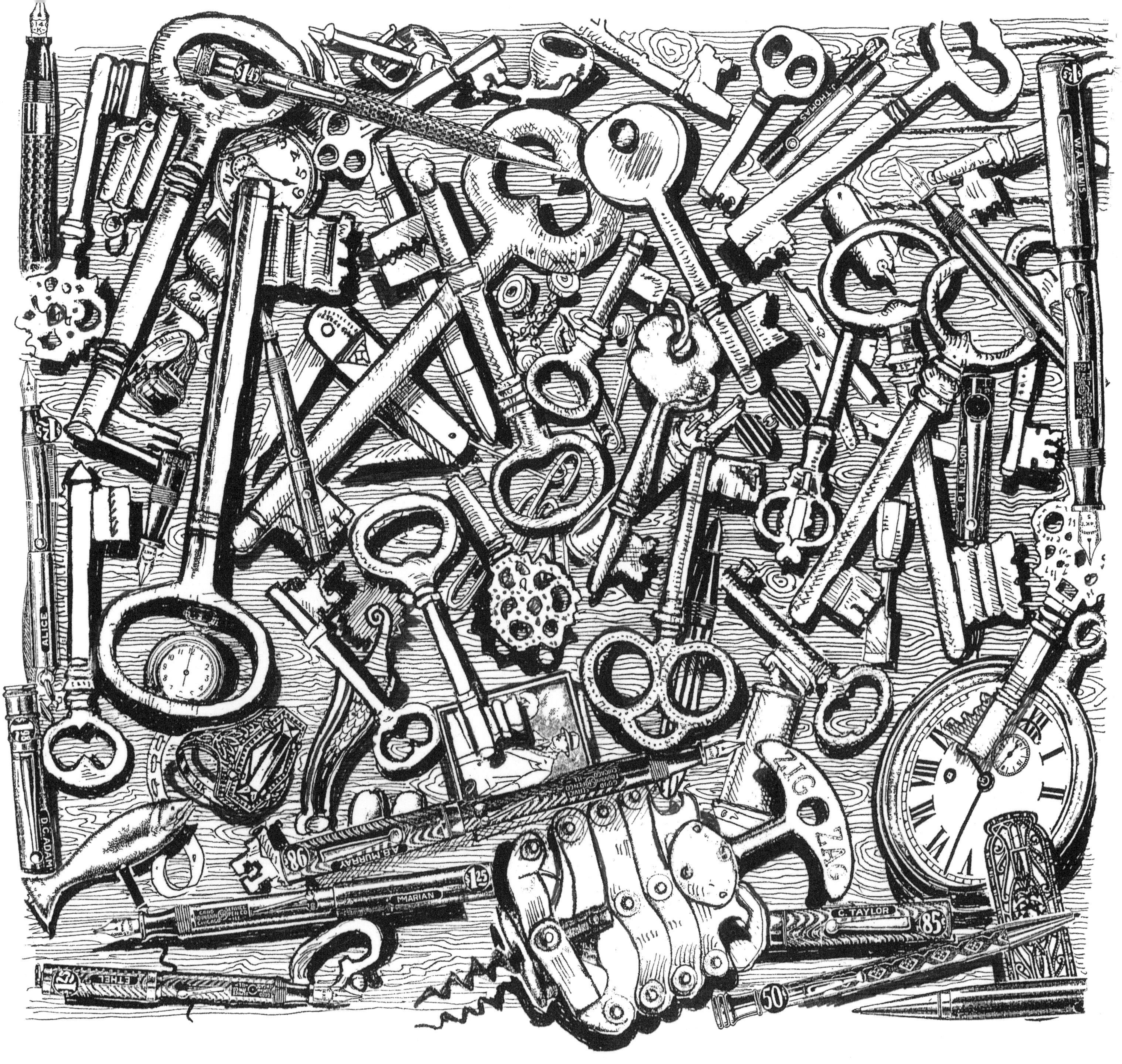

W.A. LEWIS
J. THOMAS
P.L. NELSON
ALICE
A.B. MURRAY
C. TAYLOR
ETHEL
ZIG ZAG

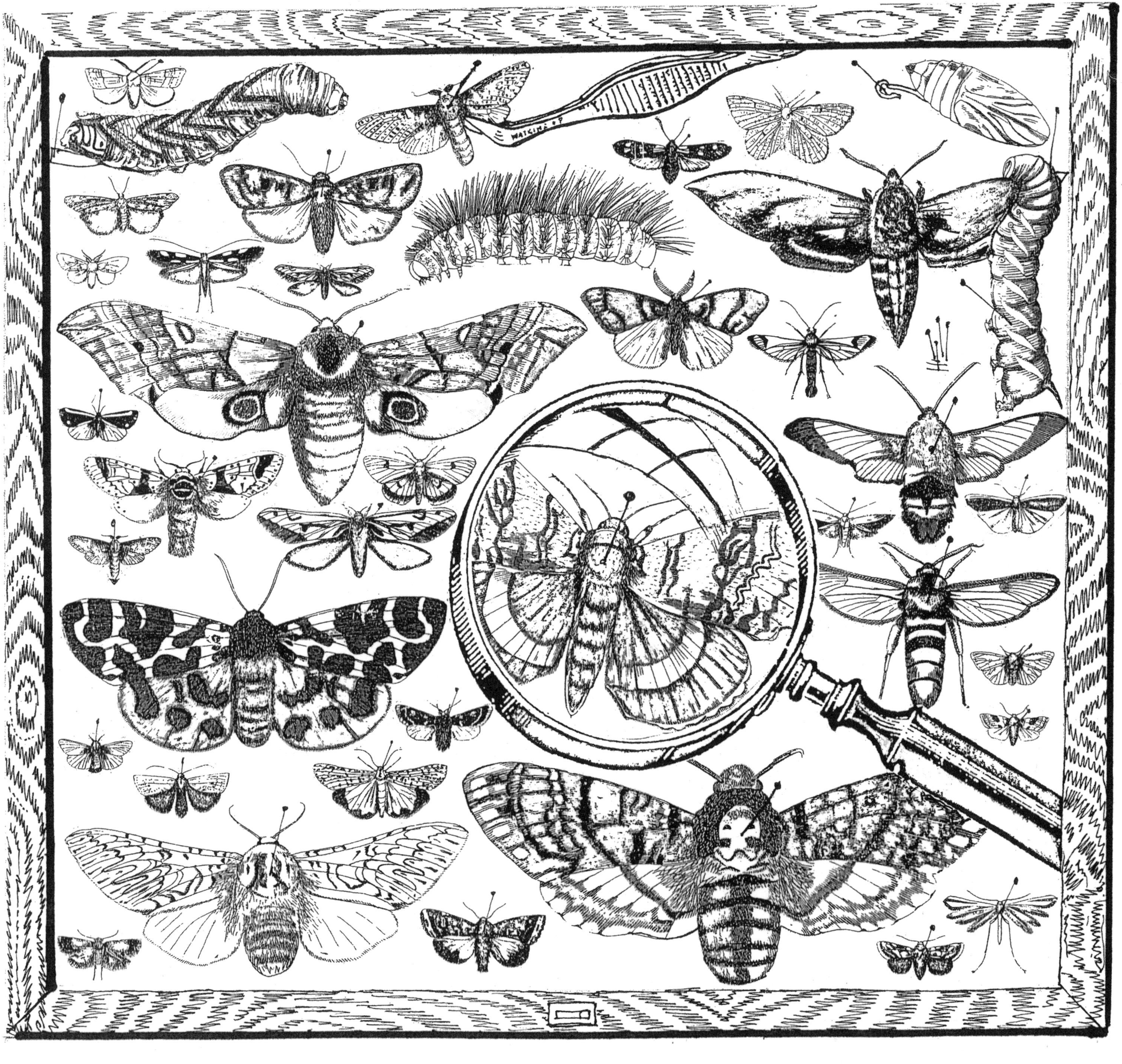

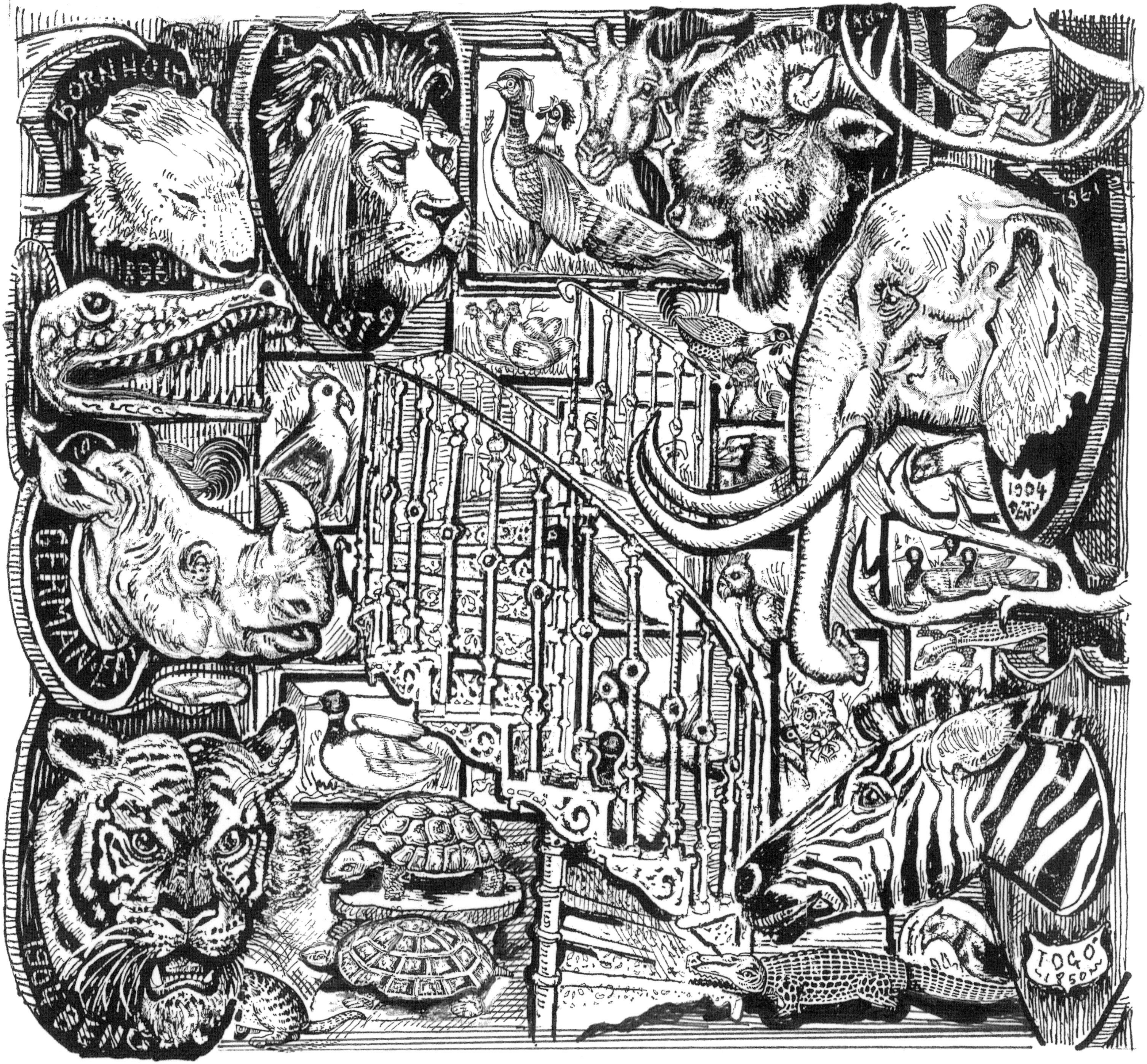
1879
1904
TOGO
1850

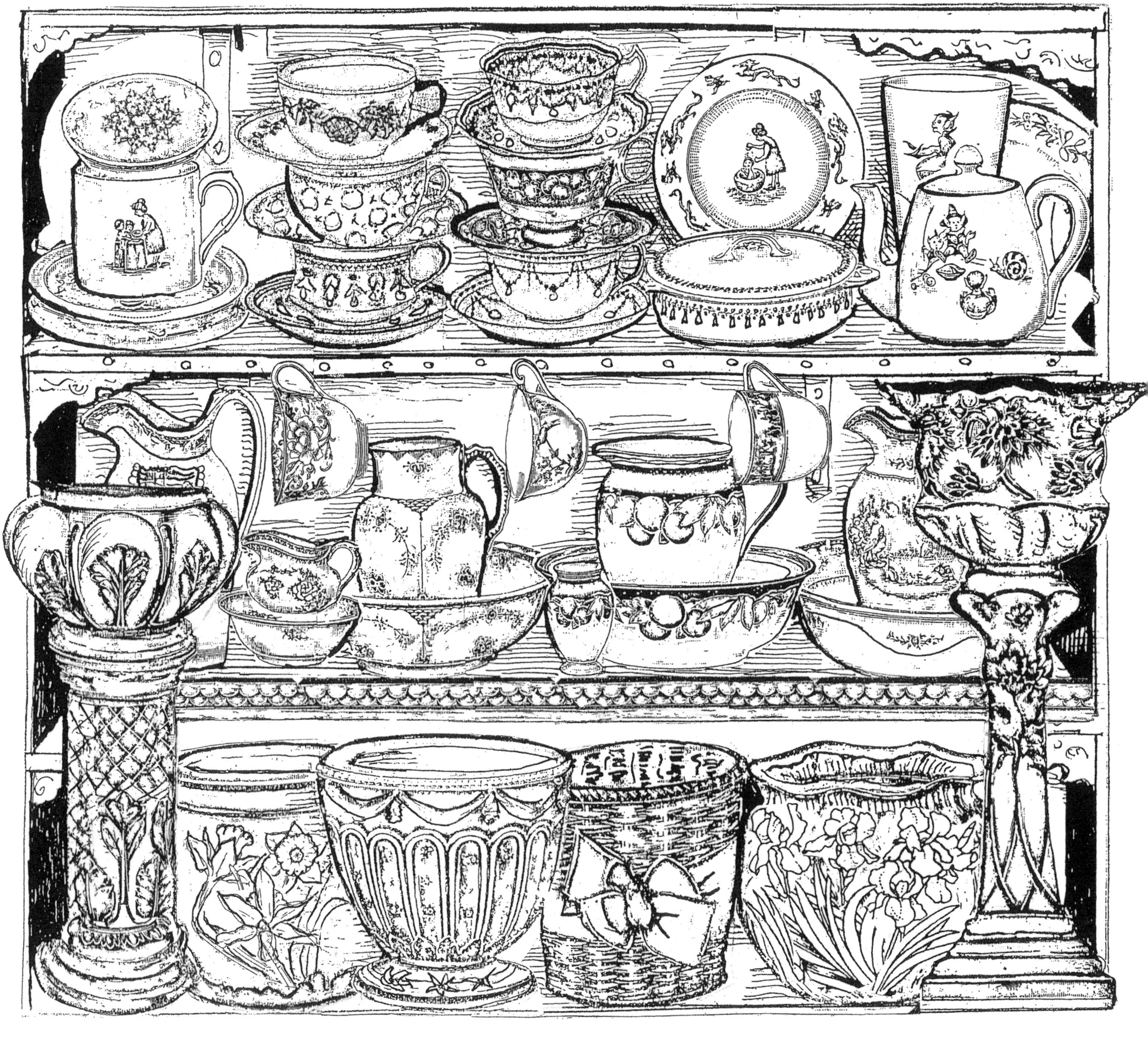

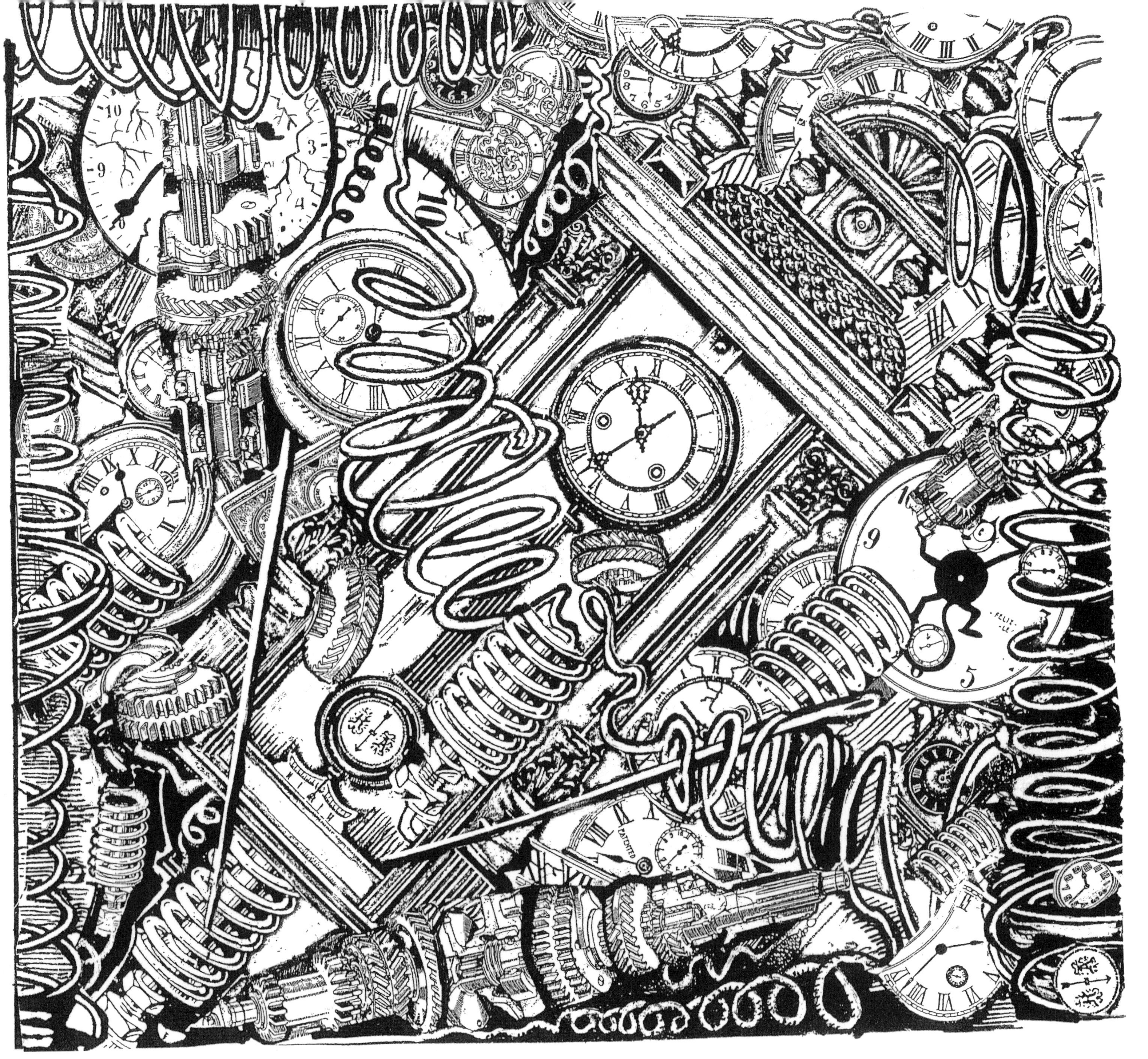

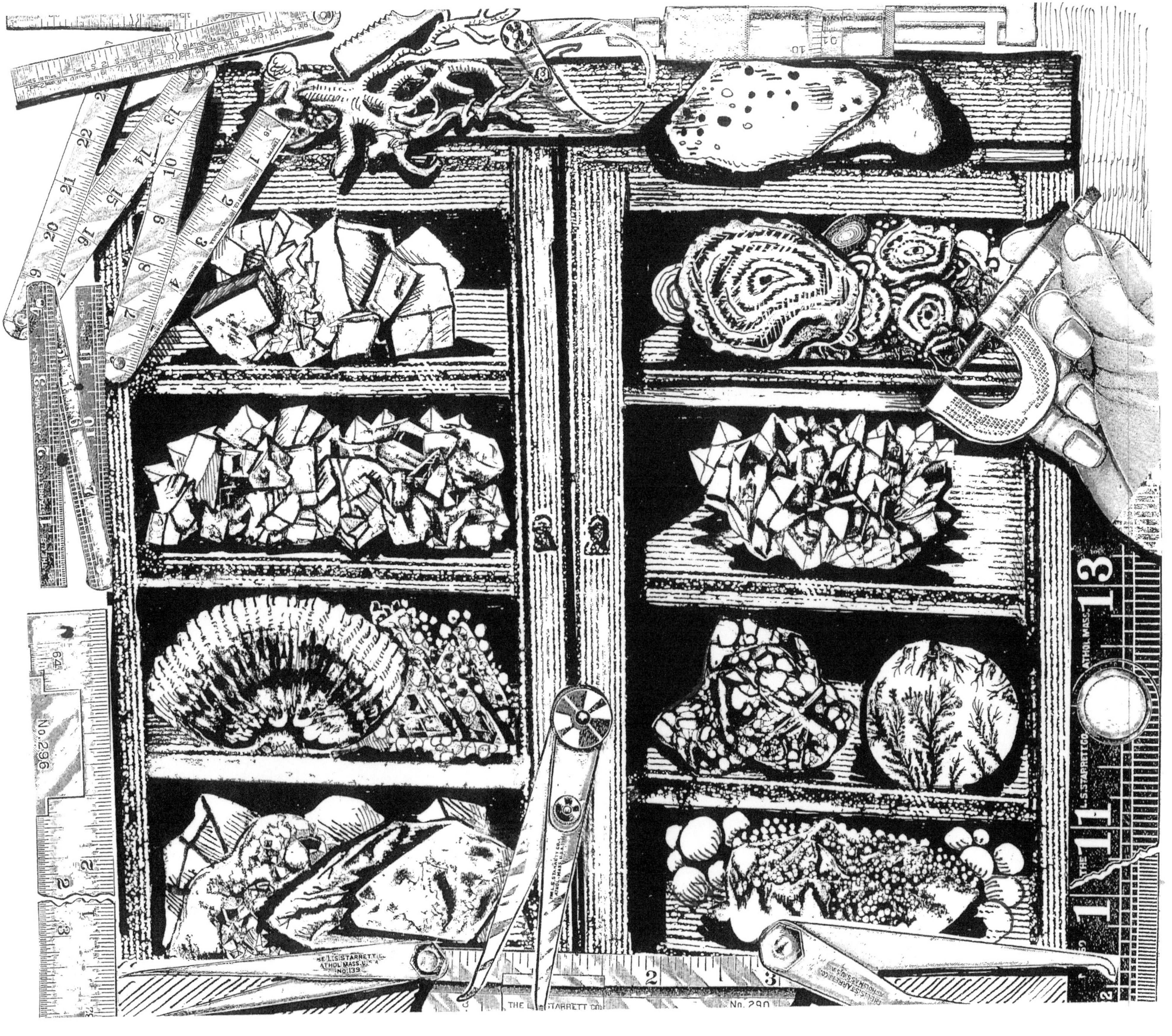

No. 296
ATHOL MASS.
No. 139
No. 290
13
11

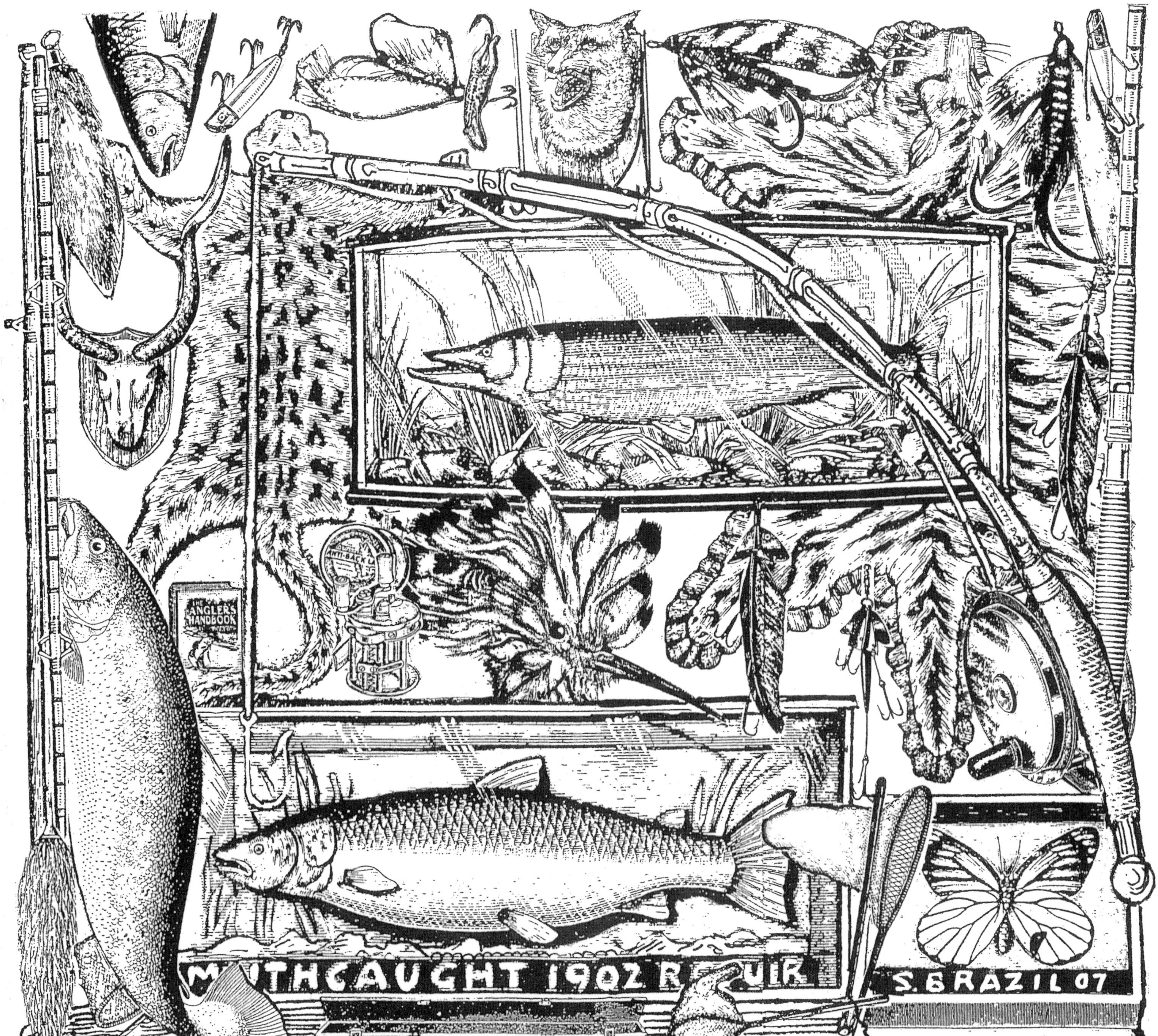
THE ANGLER'S HANDBOOK
S. BRAZIL 07

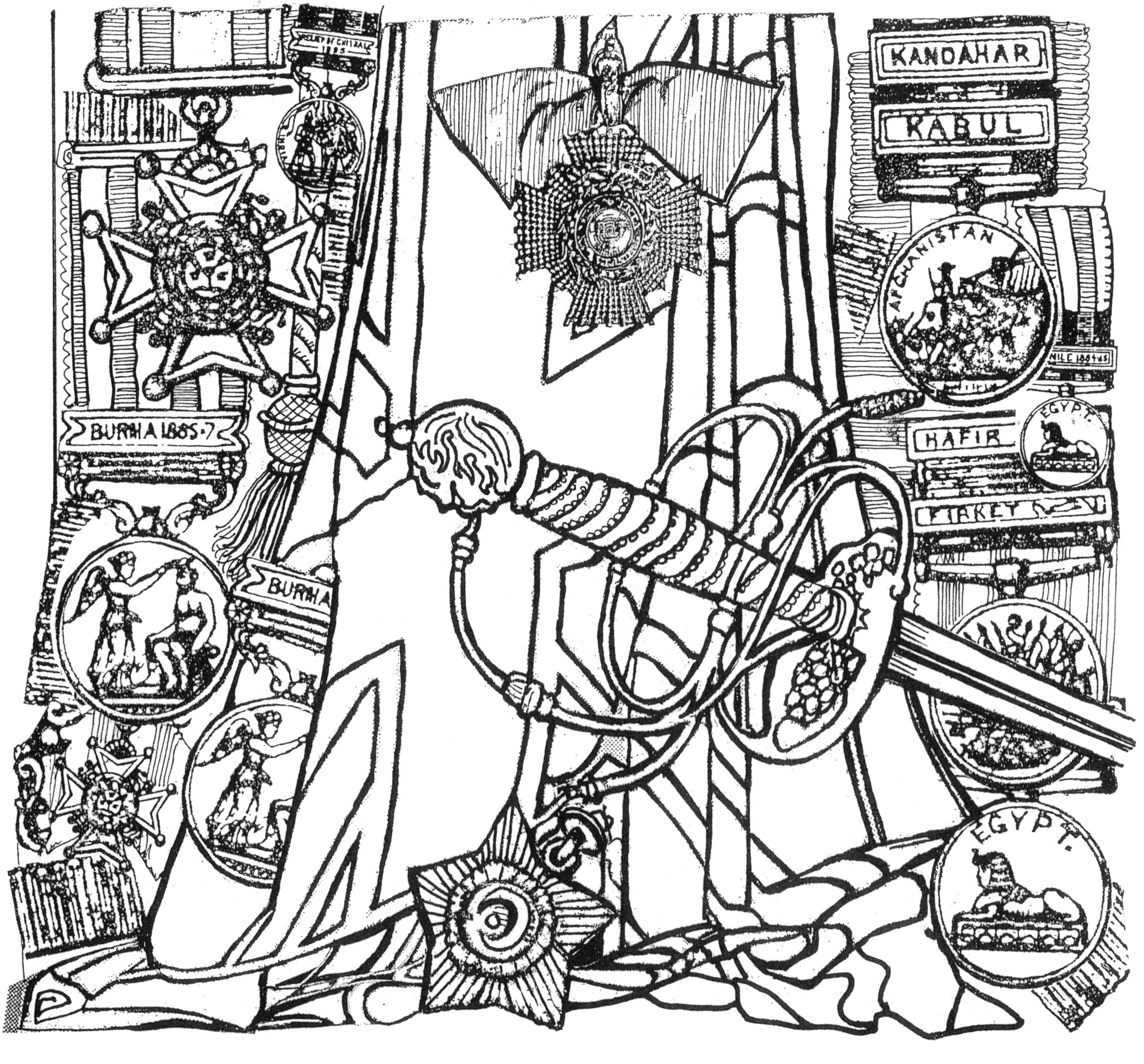

KANDAHAR
KABUL
AFGHANISTAN
NILE 1884-85
EGYPT.
HAFIR
FIRKET
BURMA 1885-7
BURMA
EGYPT.

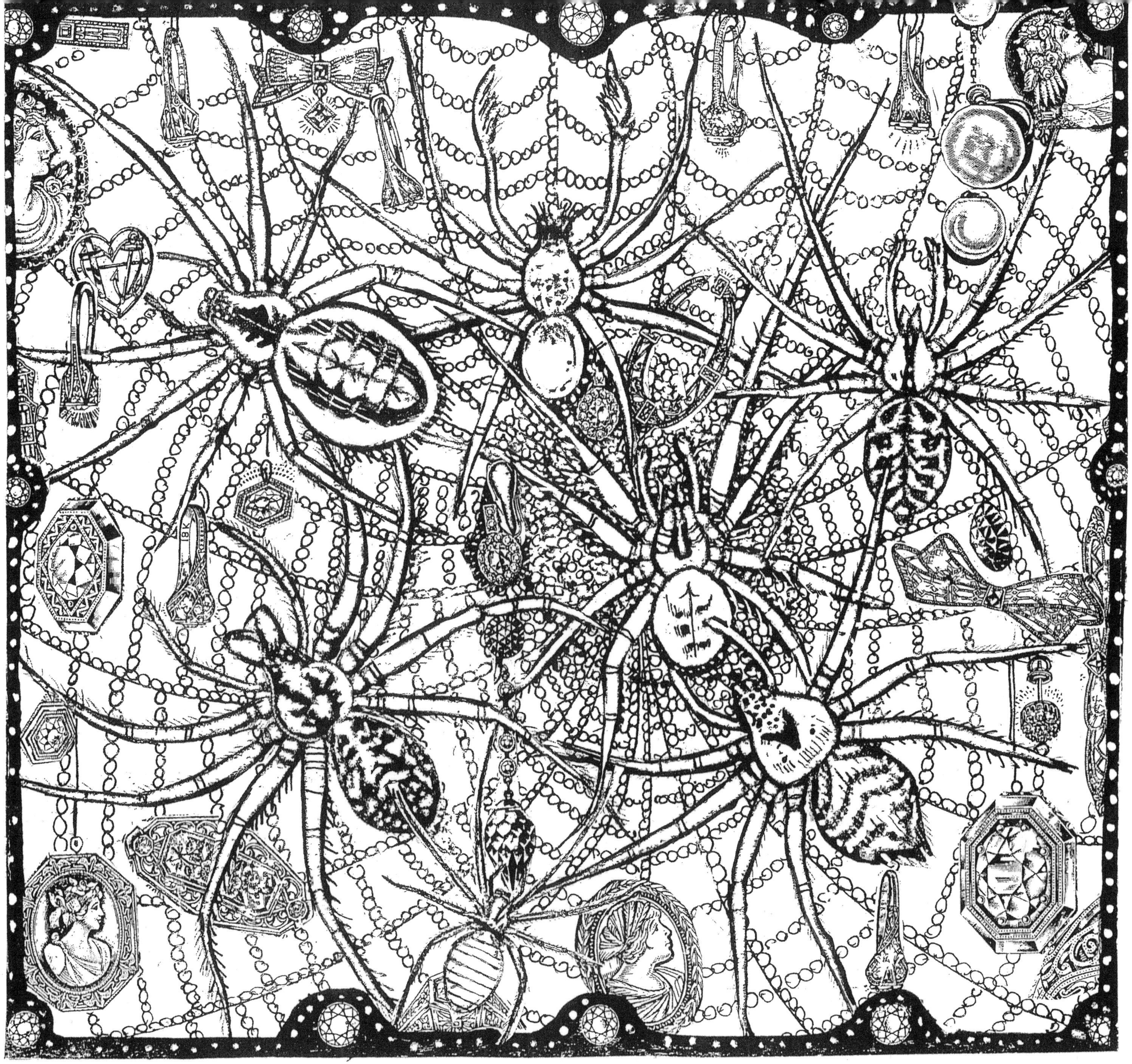
18K

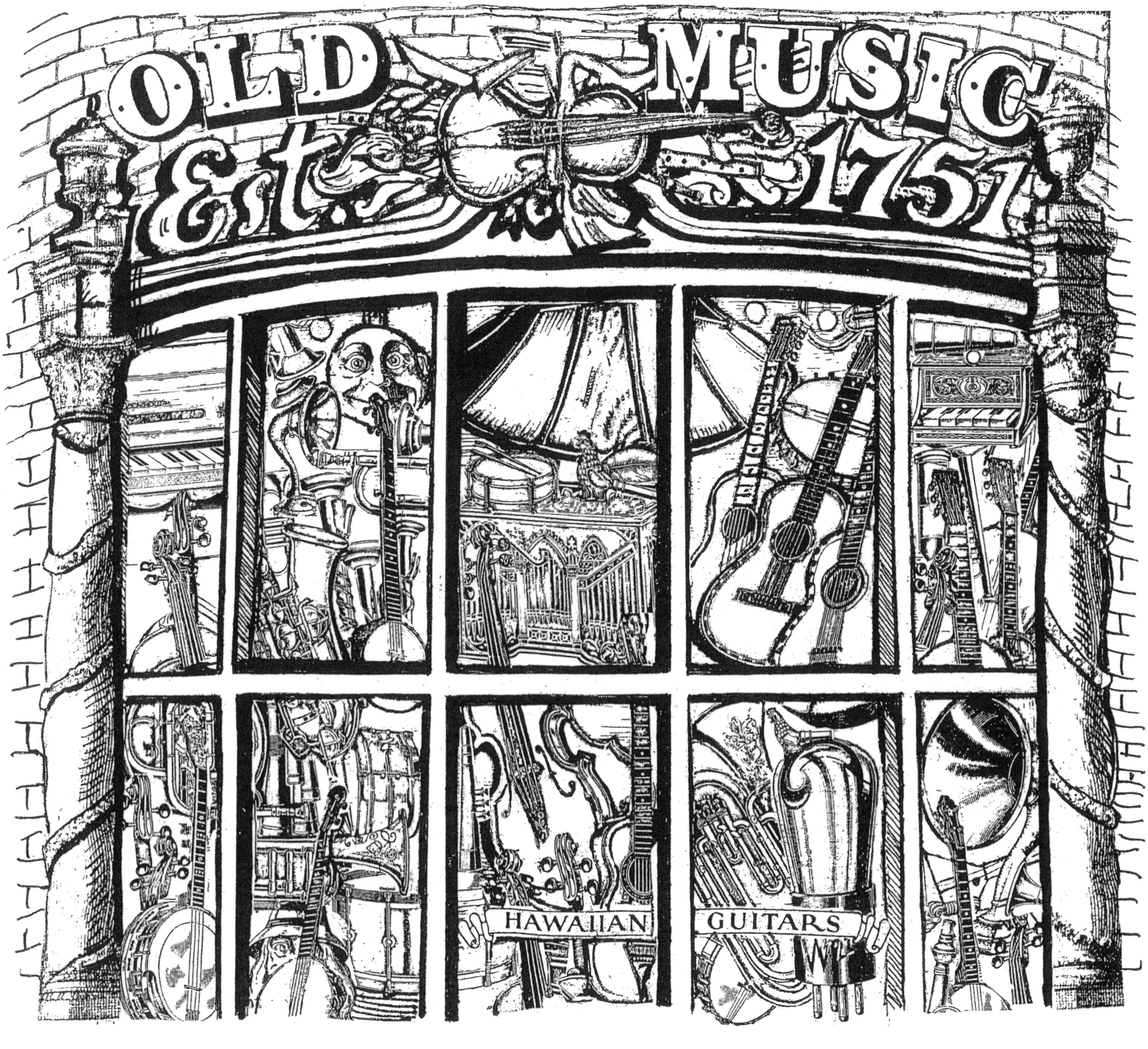
OLD MUSIC
Est. 1751
HAWAIIAN
GUITARS

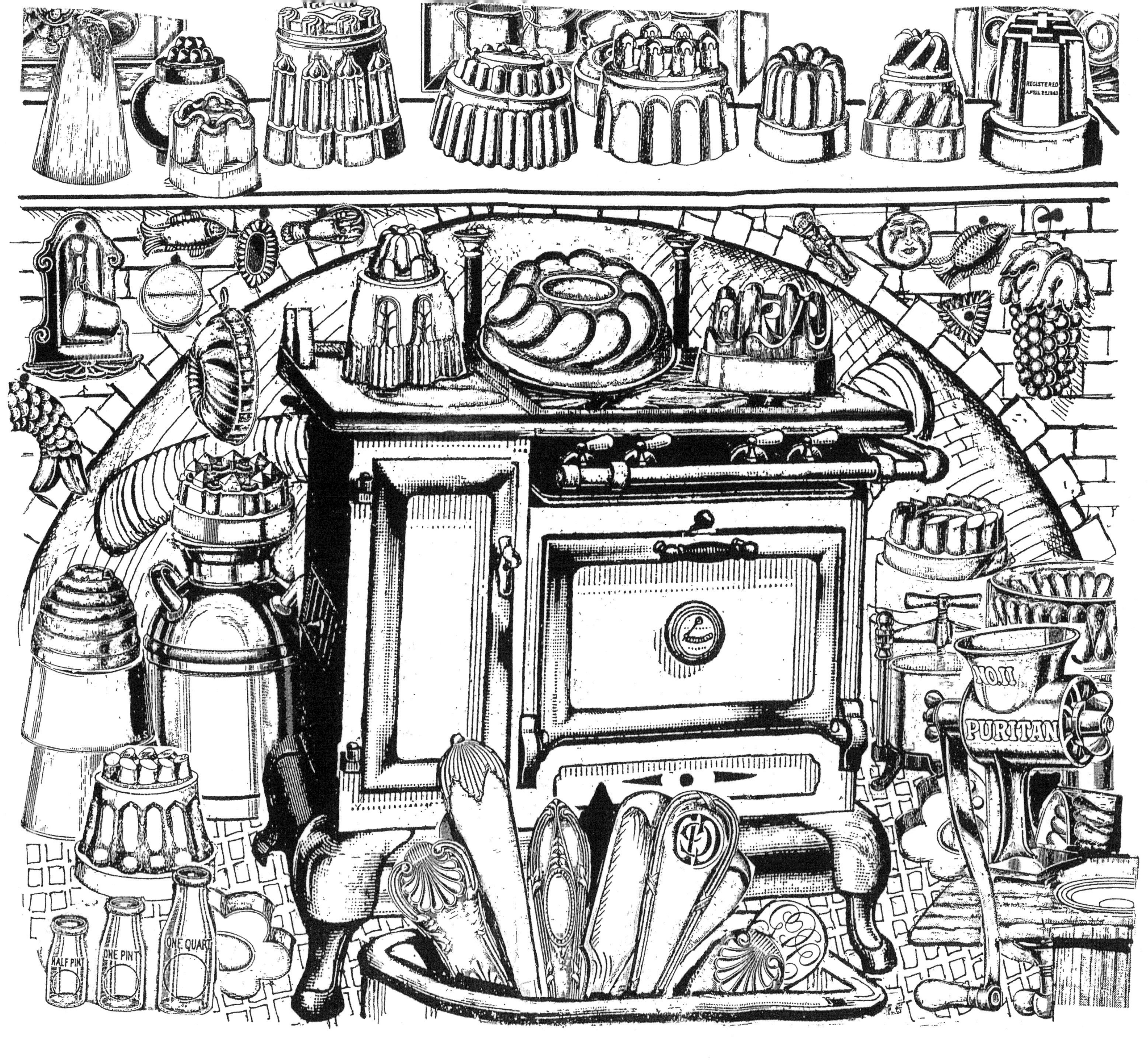

REGISTERED
PURITAN
HALF PINT
ONE PINT
ONE QUART

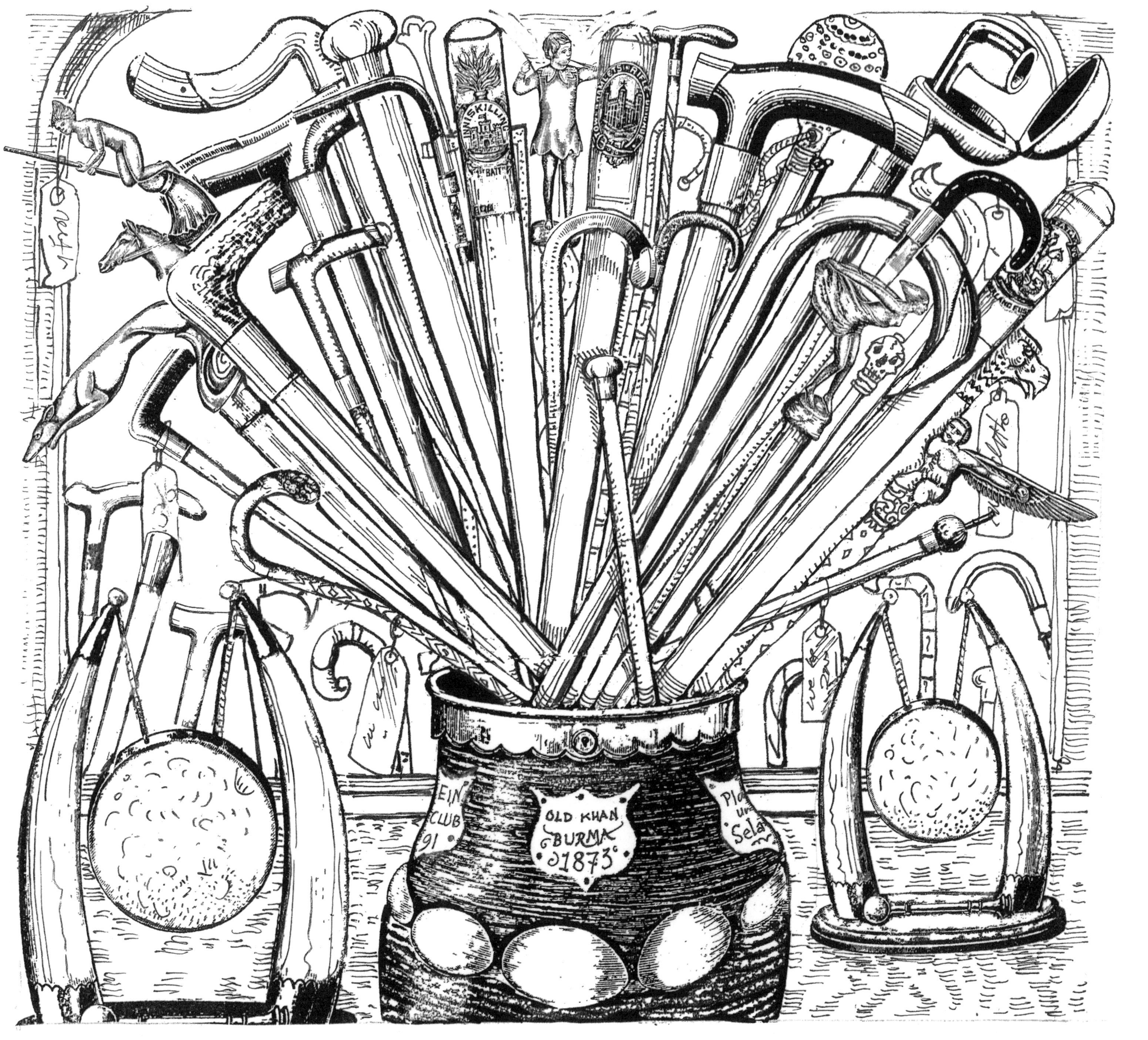
OLD KHAN
BURMA
1873

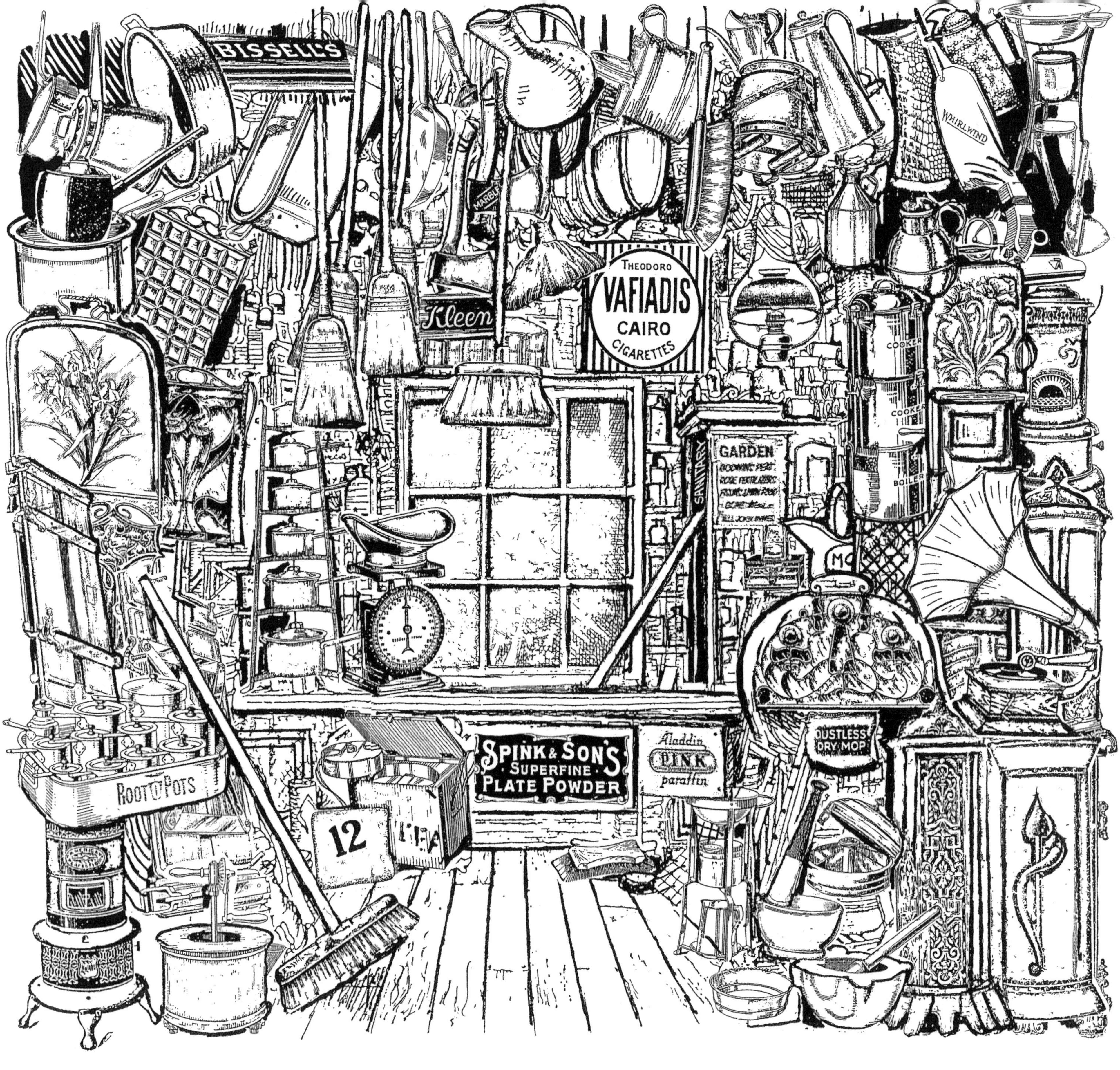
BISSELL'S
WHIRLWIND
MARBLE
Kleen
THEODORO
VAFIADIS
CAIRO
CIGARETTES
COOKER
COOKER
BOILER
SANITARY
GARDEN
DUSTLESS DRY MOP
SPINK & SON'S
SUPERFINE
PLATE POWDER
Aladdin
PINK
paraffin
12

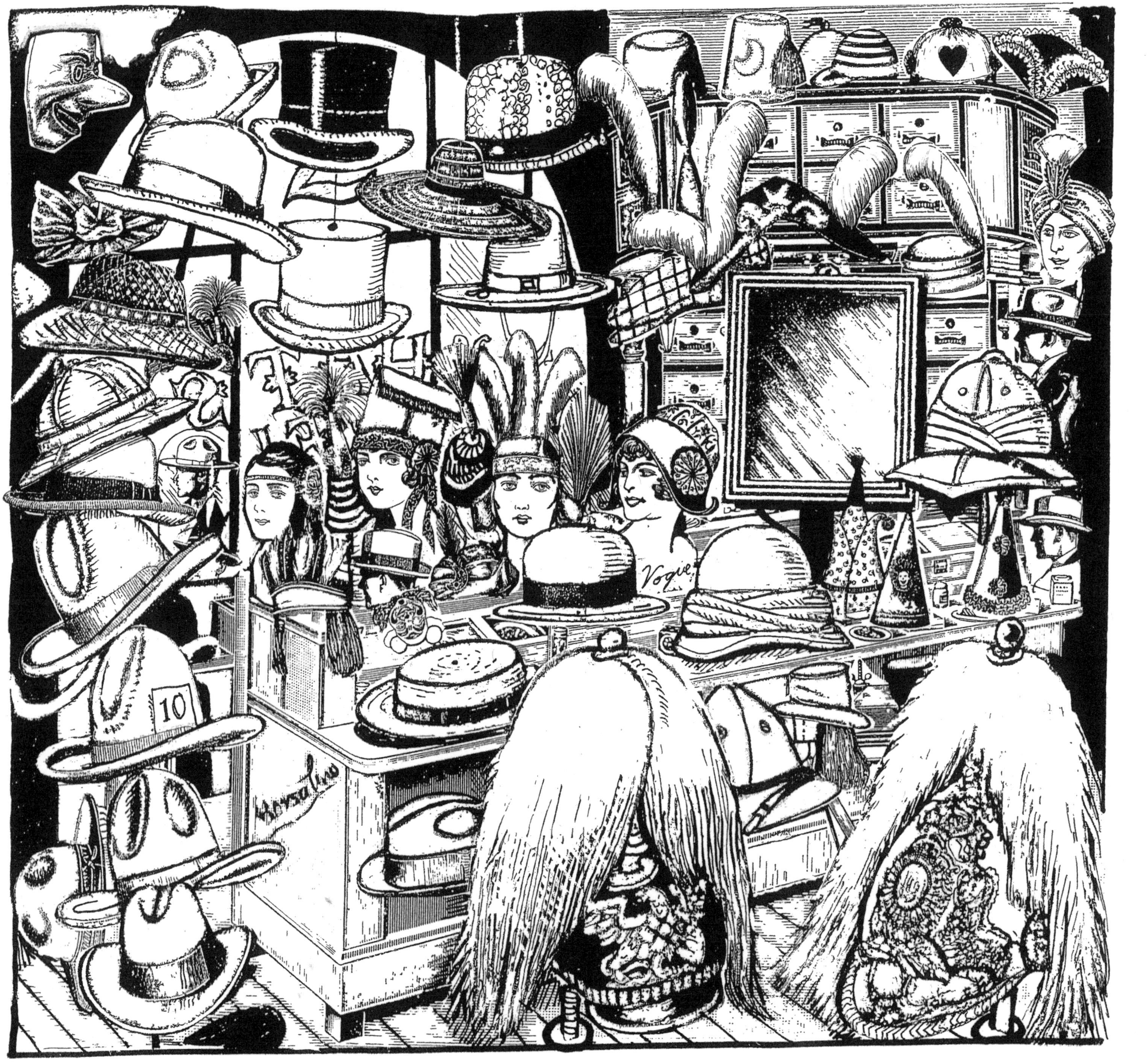
10
Vogue
Borsalino

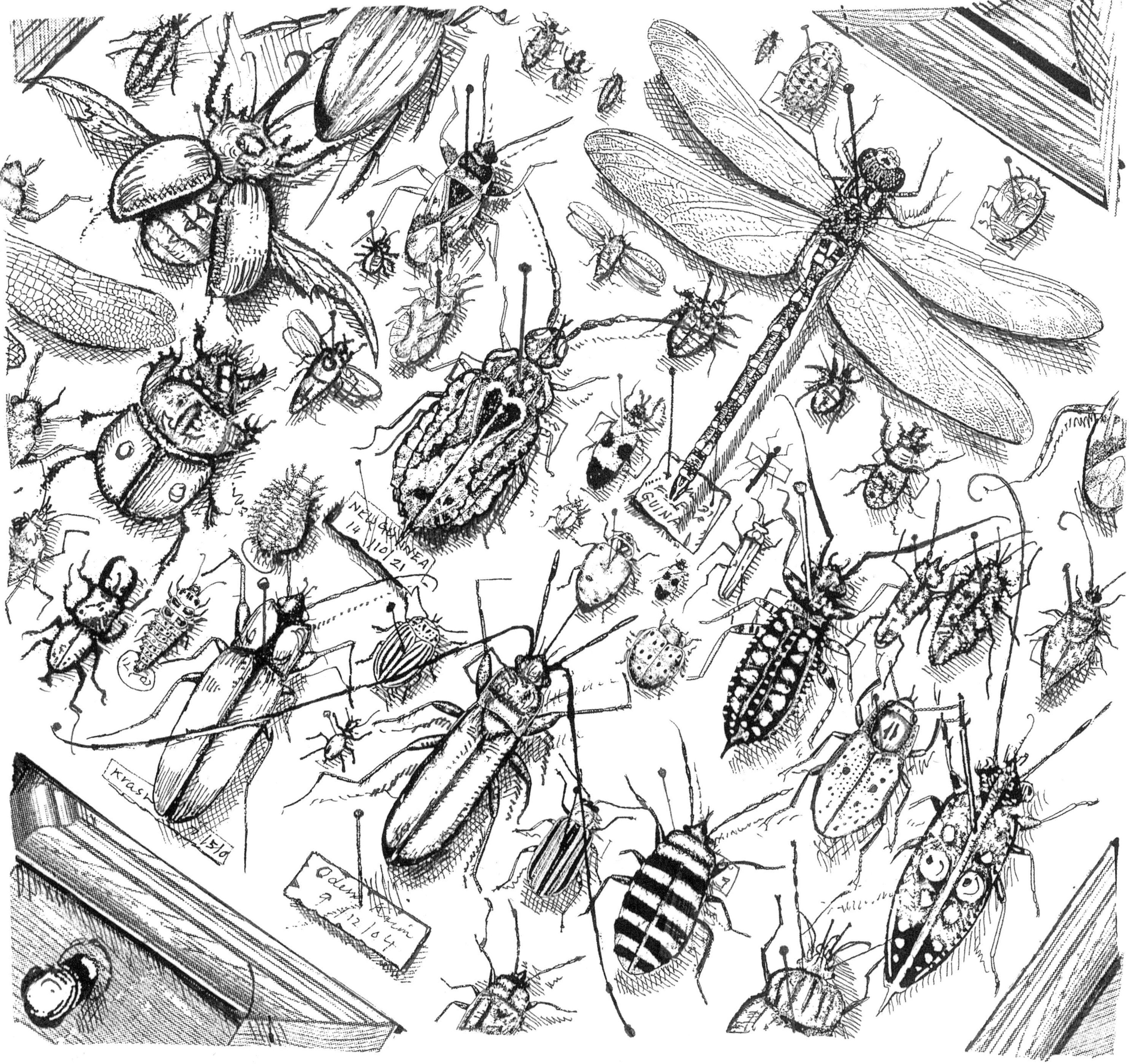

14/10/21
GUINA
Krasl

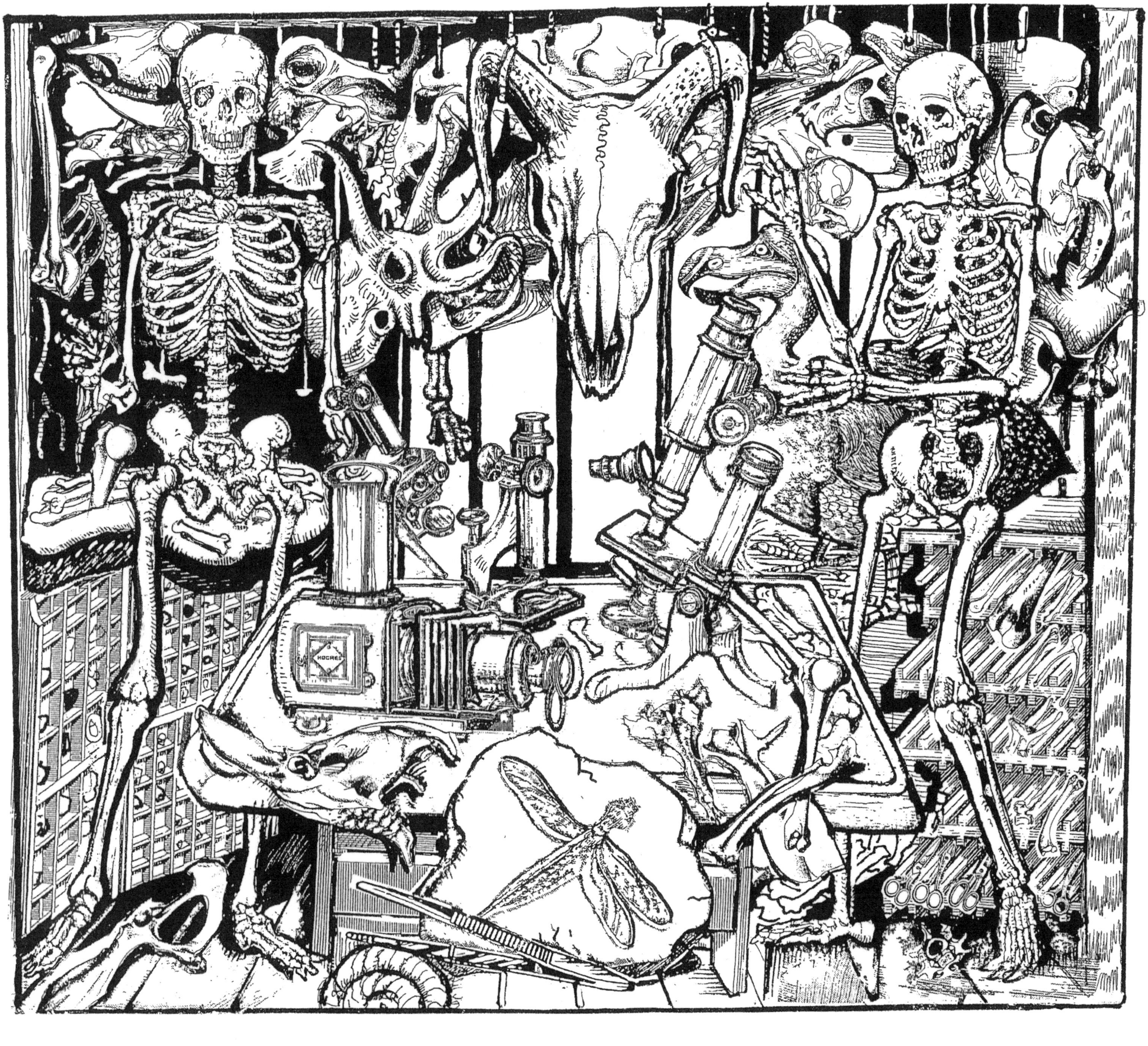
HOCRES

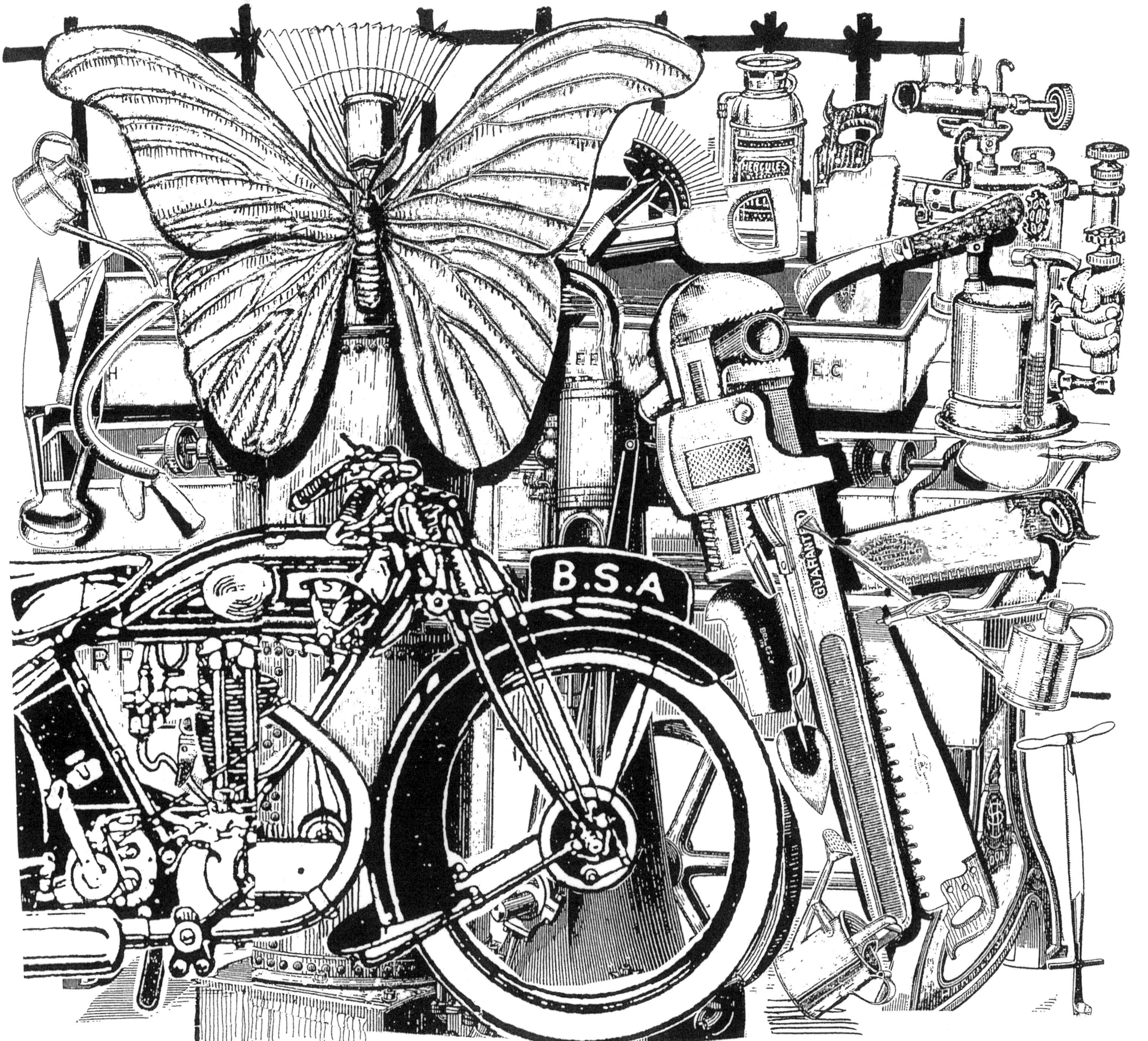
B.S.A
HERCULES

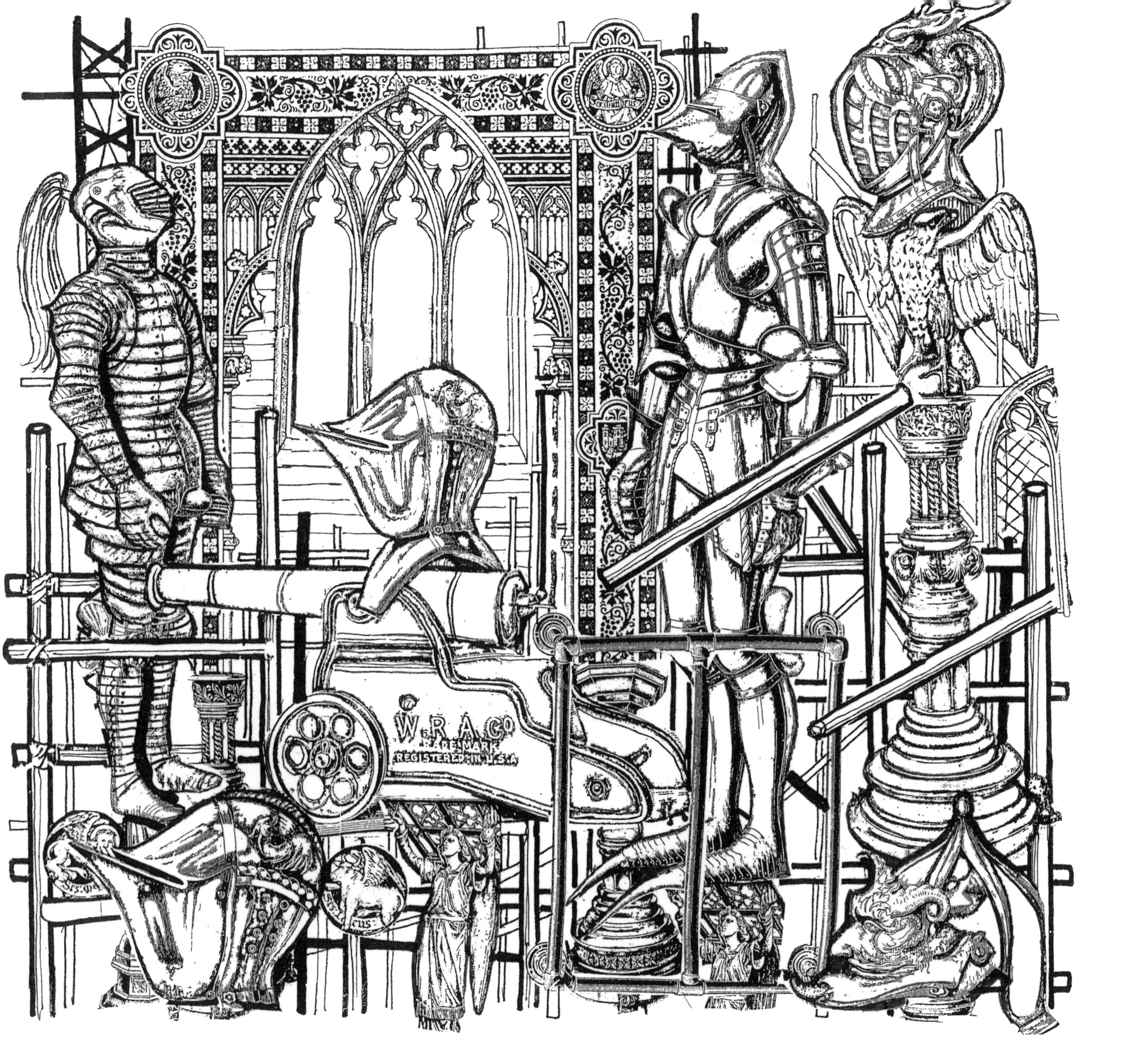
W.R.A.Co
REGISTERED IN U.S.A

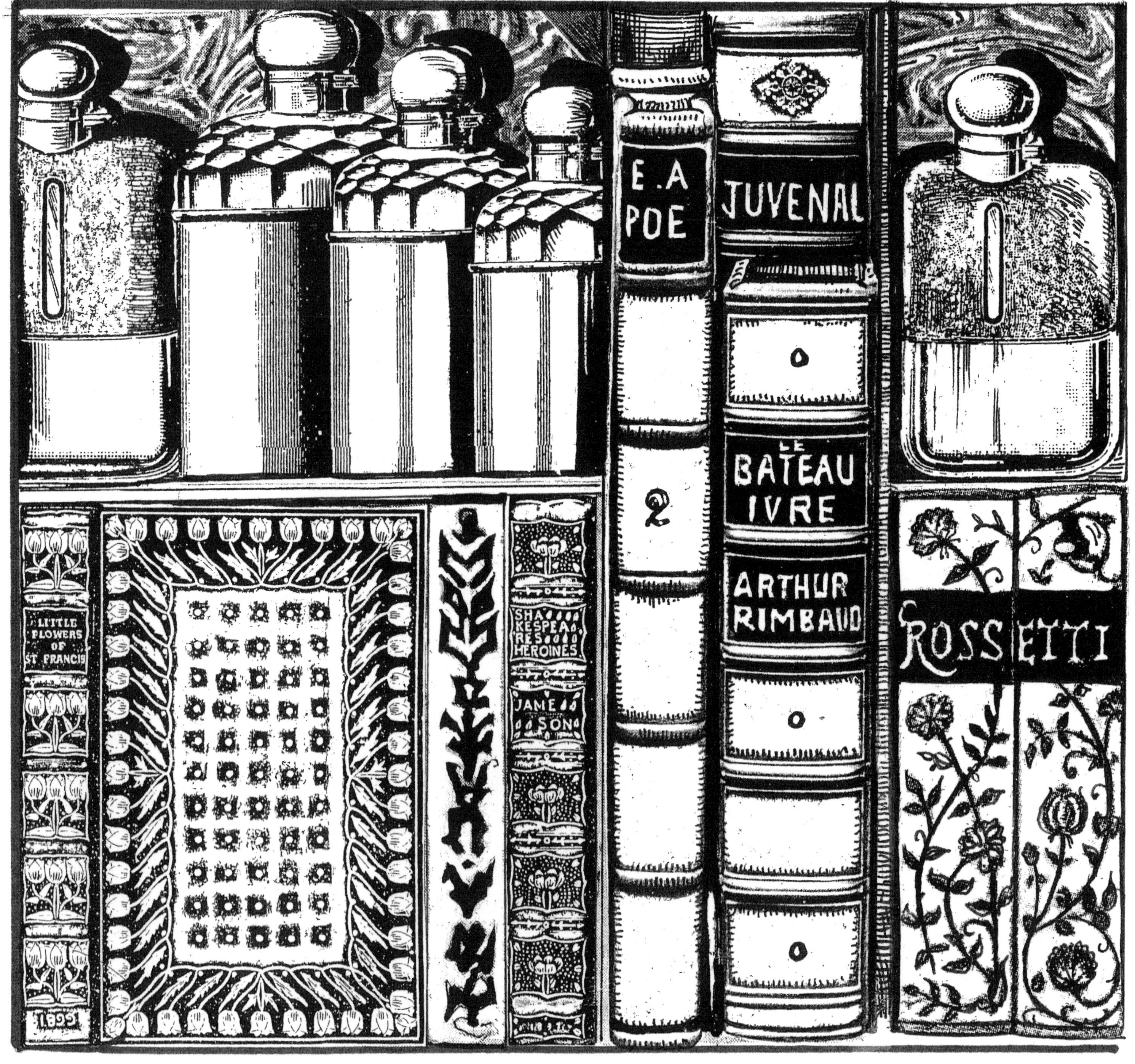

E.A
POE
JUVENAL
2
LE
BATEAU
IVRE
ARTHUR
RIMBAUD
LITTLE
FLOWERS
OF
ST. FRANCIS
SHA
KESPEA
RES
HEROINES
JAME
SON
ROSSETTI

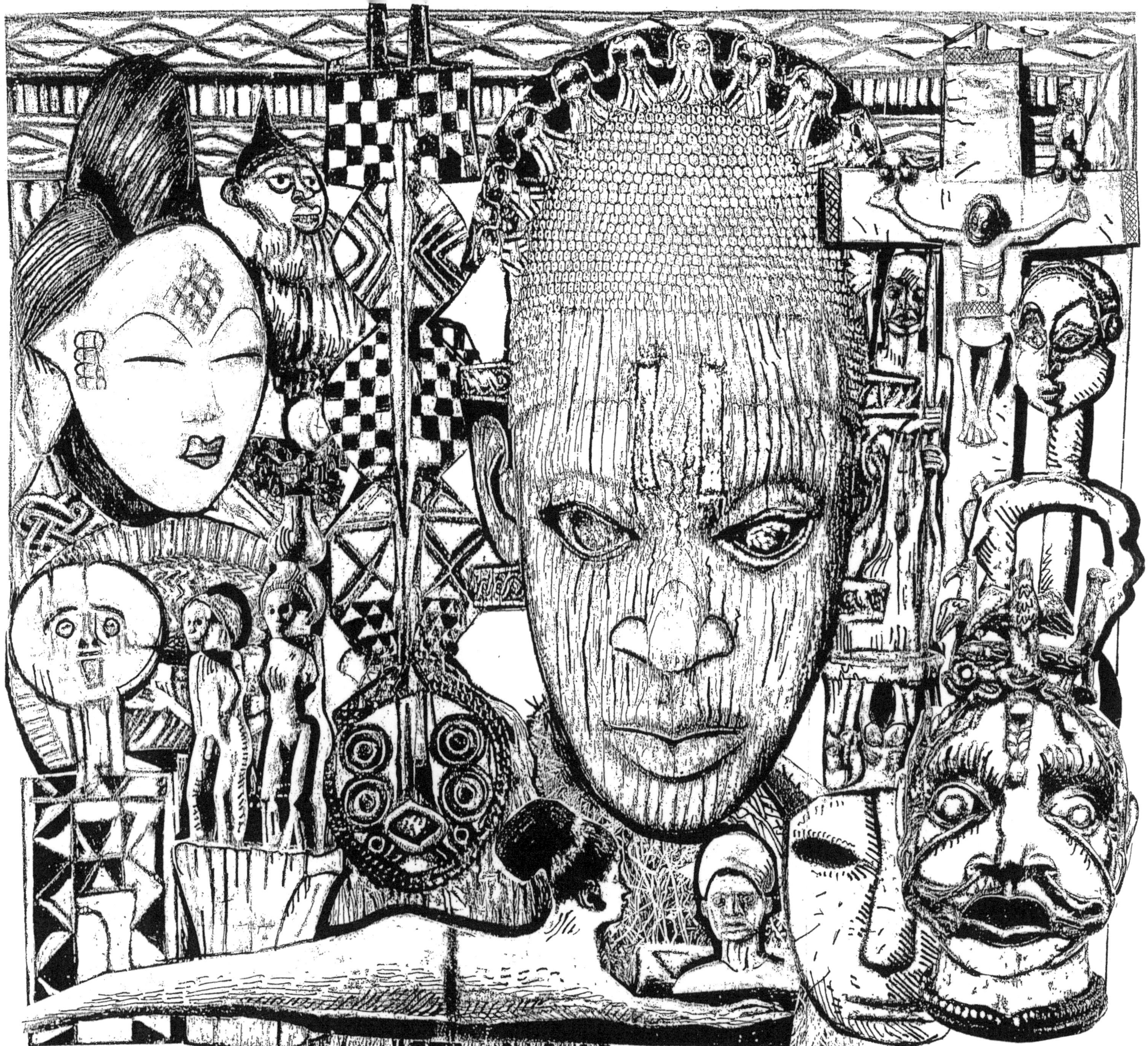

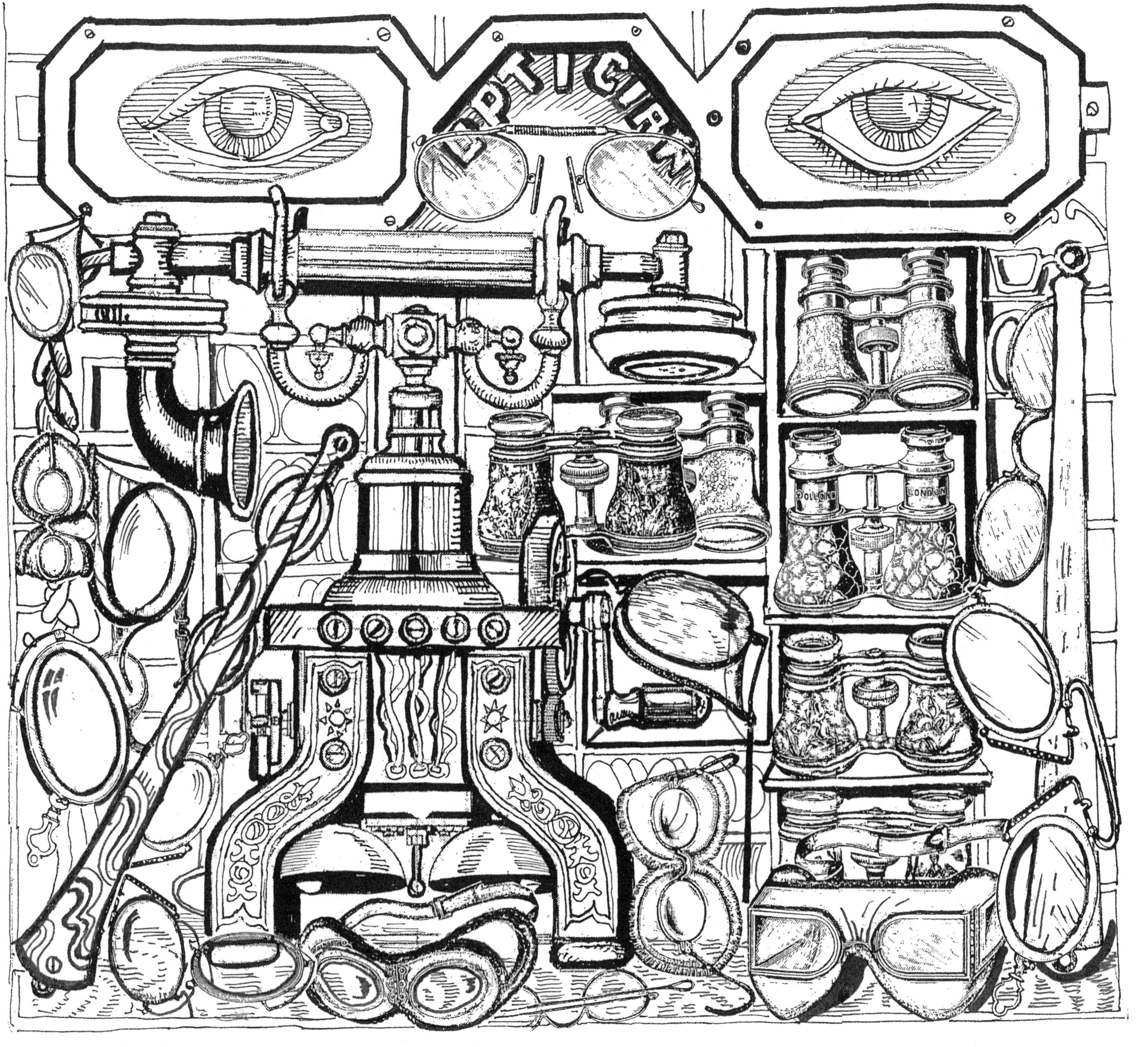
DOLLOND
LONDON